Jeff Galloway

Running

A Year
Round Plan

MEYER
& MEYER
SPORT

British Library Cataloguing in Publication Data
A catalogue record for this book is available from the British Library

Jeff Galloway
Running – A Year Round Plan
Oxford: Meyer & Meyer Sport (UK) Ltd., 2006
ISBN 10: 1-84126-169-6
ISBN 13: 978-1-84126-169-0

© 2006 by Meyer & Meyer Sport (UK) Ltd.
Aachen, Adelaide, Auckland, Budapest, Graz, Johannesburg,
New York, Olten (CH), Oxford, Singapore, Toronto
Member of the World
Sports Publishers' Association (WSPA)
www.w-s-p-a.org
Printed and bound by: TZ Verlag, Germany
ISBN 10: 1-84126-169-6
ISBN 13: 978-1-84126-169-0
E-Mail: verlag@m-m-sports.com
www.m-m-sports.com

CONTENTS

Getting Ready

The 52 Week Plan 75

What Else Do You Need to Know? 144

Jeff Galloway

Running—A Year Round Plan

WHY A
YEAR ROUND
PLAN?

Most runners like to know where they're going. For example, when running in a strange city, you'll feel more secure having a map of the route, knowing where the hills are located, with distances marked, etc. In a similar way, you'll take charge of your running destiny when you have a training plan that charts your course for the next 52 weeks.

As you schedule workouts toward your goals, you develop a growing confidence in your ability to improve. As you adjust to the training, you will head directly toward your potential and the finish line. As you schedule each running week, you become the captain of your running ship.

This book has more than the framework of a very successful strategy. First, you'll learn what is a realistic goal for you, right now. Then you will have the opportunity to train for 5K, 10K, half marathon, and marathon in one year. You may choose any of these goals or all of the above. Each week you'll have workouts that will prepare you for the next phase.

This book is written as one runner to another and is the result of about 50 years of running, several decades of speed training, and having been the "coach" to more than 150,000 runners in one way or another. None of the advice inside is offered as medical advice. To get help in this area, see a doctor or appropriate medical expert.

Motivation

Just having a plan will bestow a sense of confidence that is lacking in those who just get out there. Thousands of runners have told me that their plan kept them going when they hit a motivational lull. Even after sickness or other interruptions, the framework of your plan will give you direction. Overall, it is very motivating to become part of the process of improvement.

Each run has a purpose. Like pieces of a puzzle, the completion of the daily workout gradually fills in the overall vision of your running life. The early workouts stimulate the muscles to make gentle adaptations which prepare the body to work harder weeks or months later.

The non running days are as important as the hard workouts, providing time for the muscles, etc., to rebuild and improve internal engineering. As you look over your plan for the next few months, you'll realize that you are moving forward, while connected with your running past, heading for the future.

Planning pays off

You're more likely to achieve your potential if you use a plan. I've talked to thousands of runners who trained for years and couldn't seem to improve on a consistent basis. They had done the long runs and speed sessions—but without writing anything down or ensuring regularity. Then, during one season with a plan they improved 10, 20, even 30 minutes in a marathon.

Controlling injuries

The primary reason runners improve is that they stay injury free. By balancing stress with rest, you can control the gradual increases—and prevent injury. By making adjustments at the first signs of possible injury, you'll avoid a much greater period of down time, later.

Fine-tuning from previous years

As you go through the first "campaign" toward a goal, you'll help yourself greatly by tracking the adjustments (writing in the margins, etc.). As you embark on another goal in future years, you'll have a better blueprint, because you've improved the original plan through adjustments to your reality.

I believe that a great deal of the satisfaction we receive emerges from what we do on a regular basis. I've seen many people improve their outlook on life when they use a proven plan to improve their running. Following and adjusting the plan to running success is almost always a life-changing experience, for the better.

DEFINING YOUR GOAL

As you start the setup of your plan, you'll find lots of choices. The training components listed later in this book are like an "all you can eat" buffet. Before you choose which to put on your plate, you'll need to come up with your primary and secondary goals. Following are the ones I've found to be most productive for the runners I've worked with.

At the end of this chapter I will ask you to write, in pencil, your list of goals. You will probably adjust them several times as you go through the process. My advice is to keep using a pencil—and look at the goals (your bottom line) every week.

Running enjoyment

Find a way to enjoy parts of every run—even the speed training. Most of your runs should be....mostly enjoyable. You increase the pleasure by ensuring that there are social or scenic runs every week. Too often, these are the ones that are left out. Take control of your running enjoyment by scheduling the fun sessions first.

Stay injury free

When injured runners review their journal, they often find the causes of aches and pains. Make a list of past problems, and problems that pop up, and after reading the injury section of this book, make the needed adjustments. As you eliminate the injury stress, you can eliminate most of your injuries.

Avoiding overuse or burnout

All of us get the warning signs of over-training. Unfortunately, we often ignore these or don't know what they are. Your training journal is a wonderful tool for noting any possible ache, pain, loss of desire, unusual fatigue that lingers, etc. If you develop an injury, you can review your journal and often find the reasons. This helps you to become more sensitive to possible problems and make conservative adjustments in the plan to reduce injury risk.

Time goals

Those who have not finished a race of any distance, would be best advised to Choose the "A" program during the first training cycle. After finishing one marathon, for example, it would be fine to run faster in the next one. There is a steep learning curve during the initial campaign, so make it as easy on yourself as possible.

What is a realistic goal for you?

The next chapters will answer this question. You'll be introduced to a test that can tell you what you're capable of running in several events. Then, you'll learn how to choose the amount of improvement you want to shoot for.

Priority drill

Ok, it's your turn: List your current running goals, in order of their importance

1. Stay injury + fatigue free
2. Have fun
3. Get back to ultra distance
4.
5.

PRIMARY AND SECONDARY GOALS

Your first mission is to decide upon a primary goal for the year. Much of the year will build toward this, your final exam. The secondary goals can be just as important, and just as challenging. They will also prepare you for the prime goal.

Some want one goal

A high percentage of the runners I've worked with start the year with one primary goal. But once they get into a coordinated schedule of workouts and races for other goals, the benefits speak for themselves. Running becomes more interesting.

Many discover that they have more talent in races that were new to them. Even if the primary goal remains supreme, the conditioning and form improvements gained from other events prepare for the "main event."

Others like a variety of goals

The 52 week plan has such variety that it is hard to get bored. Each week you'll know exactly how many weeks you have left toward the current race goal, and when you will shift toward the following one. If one goal doesn't pan out, there are several others to come.

If you just want structure...

Some runners just want a plan to follow, every week, and like to have regular feedback on how they are running. The 52 week plan does this. If this is your choice, I suggest that you select one or two of the goal race options and focus on these to add structure to your year. Many runners in this category start the year without a goal but by week 20, are into the quest for time improvement on several fronts. You don't have to make many goal decisions in the beginning. Just start the plan, and make the choice later.

Write your primary and secondary goals on the 52 week plan, and your journal

Once you have decided on your primary goal (and secondary goals) for this year, copy the 52 week plan and note the goals on the appropriate weeks. For example, top priority is often time improvement in the marathon. But look at the other goal race options on the plan and pick one or more. Next, take your journal and write down the important workouts leading up to the primary goal.

Track your performances in "test races"

These are scheduled in the 52 week plan. It helps to have a chart on your wall or refrigerator to track how you are doing. You'll be using the prediction formulas in the next chapter.

Primary mission	Test race distance
Marathon	1 mile & 5K
Half Marathon	1 mile & 5K
10K	1 mile
5K	1 mile

THE GALLOWAY

RUN-WALK-RUN
METHOD

"Walk breaks let you control the amount of fatigue on your legs"

I doubt that you will find any training component that will help you in more ways than my run-walk-run™ method. I continue to be amazed, every week, at the reports of how these strategic walks helped runners have a wonderful experience as they improve their finish time. When placed appropriately for the individual, fatigue is erased, motivation improves, running enjoyment is enhanced, and the runner feels confident of finishing with strength. Here's how it works.

Walk before you get tired

Most of us, even when untrained, can walk for several miles before fatigue sets in, because walking is an activity that we are bio-engineered to do for hours. Running is more work, because you have to lift your body off the ground and then absorb the shock of the landing, over and over.

This is why the continuous use of the running muscles will produce fatigue, aches, and pains much more quickly. If you walk before your running muscles start to get tired, you allow the muscle to recover instantly—increasing your capacity for exercise while reducing the chance of next-day soreness.

The "method" part involves having a strategy. By using a ratio of running and walking you will manage your fatigue. Using this fatigue-reduction tool early gives you the muscle resources and the mental confidence to cope with any challenges that can come later. Even when you don't need the extra strength and resiliency bestowed by the method, you will feel better during and after your run, and finish knowing that you could have gone further.

"The run-walk method is very simple: you run for a short segment and then take a walk break, and keep repeating this pattern."

Walk breaks allow you to take control over fatigue, in advance, so that you can enjoy every run. By taking them early and often you can feel strong, even after a run that is very long for you. Beginners will alternate very short run segments with short walks. Even elite runners find that walk breaks on long runs allow them to recover faster. There is no need to be exhausted at the end of a run—even a 30 miler.

Walk breaks....

- Give you control over the way you feel at the end
- Erase fatigue
- Push back your fatigue wall
- Allow for endorphins to collect during each walk break—you feel good!
- Break up the distance into manageable units. ("two more minutes")
- Speed recovery
- Reduce the chance of aches, pains and injury
- Allow you to feel good afterward—carrying on the rest of your day without debilitating fatigue
- Give you all of the endurance of the distance of each session—without the pain
- Allow older runners or heavier runners to recover fast, and feel as good or better than the younger (slimmer) days

A short and gentle walking stride

It's better to walk slowly, with a short stride. There has been some irritation of the shins, when runners or walkers maintain a stride that is too long. Relax and enjoy the walk.

No need to ever eliminate the walk breaks

Some beginners assume that they must work toward the day when they don't have to take any walk breaks at all. This is up to the individual, but is not recommended. Remember that you decide what ratio of run-walk-run to use. There is no rule that requires you to hold to any ratio on a given day. As you adjust the run-walk to how you feel, you gain control over your fatigue.

I've run for about 50 years, and I enjoy running more than ever because of walk breaks. Each run I take energizes my day. I would not be able to run almost every day if I didn't insert the walk breaks early and often. I start most runs taking a short walk break every minute. By 2 miles I am usually walking every 3-4 minutes. By 5 miles the ratio often goes to every 7-10 minutes. But there are days every year when I stay at 3 minutes and even a few days at 1 min.

How to keep track of the walk breaks

There are several watches which can be set to beep when it's time to walk, and then beep again when it's time to start up again. Check our website (www.jeffgalloway.com) or a good running store for advice in this area.

PREDICTING RACE PERFORMANCE

In this chapter you'll learn what goals are realistic for you, how much improvement can be expected, and whether you are on track for the goal at various points. At the end of the program these scheduled tests will predict the performance you can expect on a good day, and how to make adjustments for temperature.

Regular testing takes the guesswork out of goal setting. This often involves putting reins on your ego, which will often try to talk you into goals that are not within your current capabilities. The tests allow you to adjust your workouts, and to avoid disappointment from pursuing unrealistic goals.

Prediction strategies

During my competitive years, and the first decade that I worked with other runners, I found a very beneficial prediction tool in **Computerized Running Training Programs** by Gerry Purdy and James Gardner. This book has been revised and re-published in print and software as **Running Trax**, by Track and Field News. This is a great resource and I highly recommend it.

Guidelines for using the formulas:

- You have done the training necessary for the goal— according to the training programs in this book

- You are not injured

- You run with an even-paced effort

- The weather on goal race day is not adverse (above 60°F, strong headwinds, heavy rain or snow, etc.)

The one mile test

The one mile test is our evaluation tool, and has been very accurate. After over 30 years of coaching over 150,000 runners, I've come up with formulas that allow you to predict even a marathon time, from running a fast one mile—for you. Here's how:

1. Go to a track, or other accurately measured course.
2. Warm up by walking for 5 minutes, then running a minute and walking a minute, then jogging an easy 800 meter (half mile or two laps around a track).
3. Do 4 acceleration-gliders. These are listed in the "Drills" chapter.
4. Walk for 3-4 minutes.
5. Run the one mile test—a hard effort—follow the walk break suggestions in this chapter.
6. On your first race, don't run all-out from the start—ease into your pace after the first half (2 laps).
7. Warm down by reversing the warm-up.
8. A school track is the best venue. Don't use a treadmill because they tend to be notoriously un-calibrated, and often tell you that you ran farther or faster than you really did.
9. On each successive test, try to adjust pace in order to run a faster time on the test.
10. Use the formula below to see what time is predicted in the goal races.

How hard should I run the test

Run the first lap slightly slower than you think you can average. Take a short walk break as noted in the walk break suggestions in this chapter. If you aren't huffing and puffing you can pick up the pace a bit on second lap. If you are huffing after the first lap, then just hold your pace on lap two.

Most runners benefit from taking a walk break after the second lap. At the end of lap 3, the walk break is optional. It is OK to be breathing hard on the last lap. If you are slowing down on the last lap, start a little slower on the next test. When you finish, you should feel like you couldn't run more than about half a lap further at that pace (if that). You may find that you don't need many walk breaks during the test—experiment and adjust.

To predict your per mile pace in longer distances from a 1 mile: (4 laps around the track)

5K: Take your one mile time and add 33 seconds

10K: Take your one mile time and multiply by 1.15

Half Marathon: Take your one mile time and multiply by 1.2

Marathon: Take your one mile time and multiply by 1.3

Example:

Mile time: 9:30 (or 9.5 minutes)

For 5K time, add 33 seconds: 10:03 is predicted mile pace for a 5K (31:10 predicted time)

For 10K time, multiply 9.5 x 1.15 = 10.952 min/mi x 6.2 (mi in a 10K) = 67.73 minutes or 1:07:44

For half marathon time multiply 9.5 x 1.2 = 11.4 min/mi x 13.1 mi = 149.34 minutes or 2:29:20

For marathon time, multiply 9.5 x 1.3 = 12.35 min/mi x 26.2 mi = 323.57 minutes or 5:23:35

One Mile Time	(add 33 sec) 5K Pace	(x 1.15) 10K Pace	(x 1.2) Half Mar.	(x 1.3) Marathon
5:00	5:33	5:45	6:00	6:30
5:30	6:03	6:19	6:37	7:09
6:00	6:33	6:54	7:12	7:48
6:30	7:03	7:25	7:48	8:28
7:00	7:33	8:03	8:24	9:06
7:30	8:03	8:37	9:00	9:45
8:00	8:33	9:12	9:36	10:24
8:30	9:03	9:46	10:12	11:03
9:00	9:33	10:21	11:48	11:42
9:30	10:03	10:55	11:24	12:21
10:00	10:33	11:30	12:00	13:00
10:30	11:03	12:04	12:36	13:39
11:00	11:33	12:39	13:12	14:18
11:30	12:03	13:19	13:48	14:57
12:00	12:33	13:48	14:24	15:36
12:30	13:03	14:22	15:00	16:15
13:00	13:33	14:57	15:36	16:54
13:30	14:03	15:31	16:12	17:33
14:00	14:33	16:06	16:48	18:12
14:30	15:03	16:38	17:24	18:51
15:00	15:33	17:15	18:00	19:30
15:30	16:03	17:49	18:36	20:09
16:00	16:33	18:24	19:12	20:48

Walk breaks during the one mile test

Pace of the race/per mi	#of seconds walking
8:00	5-10 sec every 2 laps
8:30	8-12 sec every 2 laps
9:00	10-15 sec every 2 laps
9:30	12-18 sec every 2 laps
10:00	5-8 sec every lap
10:30	7-10 sec every lap
11:00	9-12 sec every lap
11:30	10-15 sec every lap
12:00	11-16 sec every lap
12:30	12-17 sec every lap
13:00	13-18 sec every lap
13:30	14-19 sec every lap
14:00	15-20 sec every lap
14:30	16-21 sec every lap
15:00	17-22 sec every lap
15:30	18-23 sec every lap
16:00	19-24 sec every lap

The "leap of faith" goal prediction

It is OK to choose a time for your goal race which is faster than is predicted by your pre-test. As you do the speed training, the long runs and your test races, you should improve. For prediction purposes, as you take this "leap" to a goal, I suggest no more than a 3-5% improvement in a 3 month training program.

1. Run the one mile test
2. Use the formulas above to predict what you could run now, if you were trained for the goal distance
3. Choose the amount of improvement during the 52 week program (3-5%)
4. Subtract this from # 2—this is your goal time

How much of a "leap of faith"?

Pre-test prediction in the 5K	3% Improvement	5% Improvement
(Over a 2-3 month training program)		
40 minutes	1 minute 12 sec.	2 minutes
33 minutes	60 seconds	1 minute 40 sec.
28 minutes	50 seconds	1 minute 24 sec.
25 minutes	45 seconds	1 minute 15 sec.
20 minutes	36 seconds	60 seconds
17 minutes	31 seconds	51 seconds
Half marathon		
3:00	2:54:36	2:51:00
2:30	2:25:30	2:22:30
2:00	1:56:24	1:54:00
Marathon		
6:30	6:18:18	6:10:30
6:00	5:49:12	5:42:00
5:30	5:20:06	5:13:30
5:00	4:51:00	4:45:00
4:30	4:21:54	4:16:30
4:00	3:52:48	3:48:00

The key to goal setting is keeping your ego in check. From my experience, I have found that a 3% improvement is realistic. This means that if your 5K time is predicted to be 30 minutes, that it is realistic to assume that you could lower it by 54 seconds if you do the speed training and the long runs as noted on my training schedules, during the 52 week plan. Those who have been running longer (two years or more) and have not been doing speed training for more than a year, could try for a more aggressive, 5% improvement: 1 minute off a 20 minute 5K.

In all of these situations, however, everything must come together to produce the predicted result. Even runners who shoot for a 3% improvement, do all the training as described, achieve their goal slightly more than 50% of the time during a racing season. There are many factors that determine a time goal in a marathon that are outside of your control: weather, terrain, etc.

Test race

Test races are noted on the year-round schedule, every few weeks. These will help you chart your progress.

- Follow the same format as listed in the pre-test, above.
- By doing this as noted, you will learn how to pace yourself.
- Hint: it's better to start a bit more slowly than you think that you can run.
- Walk breaks will be helpful for most runners. Read the section in this book for suggested ratios.
- Note whether you are speeding up or slowing down at the end, and adjust in the next test.
- If you are not making progress then look for reasons and adjust.

Reasons why you may not be improving:

1. You're over-trained, and tired—if so, reduce your training, and/or take an extra rest day.

2. You may have chosen a goal that is too ambitious for your current ability.

3. You may have missed some of your workouts, or not been as regular with your training.

4. The temperature may have been above 60°F (15°C). Above this, you will slow down (the longer the race, the more effect heat will make on the result).

5. When using different test courses, one of them may not have been accurately measured.

6. You ran the first lap or two too fast.

Final reality check

Take the last 4 tests, and eliminate the slowest time. Average the 3 remaining times get a good prediction in your goal race. **If the tests are predicting a time that is slower than the goal you've been training for, adjust your race goal accordingly.** It is strongly recommended that you run the first one-third of your goal race a few seconds a mile slower than the pace predicted by the test average.

Use a journal!

Read the chapter on using a journal. Your chance of reaching your goal increases greatly with this very important instrument. Psychologically, you start taking responsibility for the fulfillment of your mission when you use a journal.

PREPARING

FOR THE PLAN

There are a number of running products in the next chapter which make running easier. More important than these helpful tools is your mental preparation. Be sure to read carefully the chapter above on "Primary And Secondary Goals" Above all, focus on the enjoyment of running. Virtually everyone can feel great after and during a run, and that becomes a greater reward than anything you can buy for yourself.

One of the liberating feelings you get from running comes from its simplicity—the minimal requirements. You can run from your house or office in most cases, using public streets or pedestrian walkways. Ordinary clothing works well most of the time and you don't need to join a country club or invest in expensive exercise equipment. While running with another person can be motivating, you don't have to have a partner, and most runners run alone on most of their runs. It helps, however, to have a "support team" as you go through the training (running companions, doctors, running shoe experts) but you will probably meet these folks through the running grapevine.

Medical check

Check with your doctor's office before you start a strenuous training program. And keep the doctor informed of any irregularities in your cardiovascular system or aches and pains that could be injuries. At first, just tell the Doctor or head nurse how much running you plan to be doing over the next year. Almost every person will be given the green light. If your doc recommends against your running plans, ask why. Since there are so few people who cannot train even for strenuous goals if they use a liberal run-walk-run tm formula, I suggest that you get a second opinion if your doctor tells you not to run. Certainly the tiny number of people who should not run have good reasons. But the best medical advisor is one who wants you to get the type of physical activity that engages you—unless there are significant reasons not to do so.

Note: the information in this book is offered as advice from one runner to another, and not meant to be medical advice. Having a doctor/advisor will not only help you through some problems more quickly. A responsive and supportive medical advisor will improve confidence and motivation, while reducing anxiety.

Choosing a doctor

A growing number of family practice physicians are advocates for fitness. If your doctor is not very supportive, ask the nurses in the office if there is one, in the same office group, who might be. The doctors who are physical fitness advocates are very often more positive, and energetic—and stay up with the latest research on how exercise reduces disease and prolongs the quality of life.

The running grapevine can help

Ask the staff at local running stores, running club members, or long-term runners. They will usually know of several doctors in your town who runners see when they have a problem. Doctors tell me that compared with their other patients, runners tend to ask more questions, want to keep themselves in good health, and have fewer health downturns. You want a doctor who will welcome this, and serve as your "health coach"; someone who will work *with* you to avoid injury, sickness, and other health setbacks.

Shoes: the primary investment: usually less than $100 and more than $65

Most runners decide, wisely, to spend a little time on the choice of a good running shoe. After all, shoes are the only real equipment needed. The shoe that is a good match for your feet can make running easier, while reducing blisters, foot fatigue and injuries.

Because there are so many different brands and many different models, shoe shopping can be confusing. The best advice....is to get the best advice. Going to a good running store, staffed by helpful and knowledgeable runners, can cut the time required and can usually lead you to a better shoe choice than you would find for yourself. For more information on this see *Galloways Book On Running, 2nd Edition*, and the back section of this book.

Buy the training shoe first

Go to the running store in your area with the most experienced staff. First you'll need a pair for long runs and easy running days. You may want to get a racing shoe (or light weight training shoe) later.

Bring along your most worn pair of shoes (any shoes), and a pair of running shoes that has worked well for you. Wait until you are several weeks into your training before you decide to get a racing shoe if you feel you need one.

Do I need a racing shoe?

In most cases, racing shoes only speed you up by a few seconds a mile—but this may be what you need to reach your goal. After several weeks, if you feel that your training shoes are too heavy or "clunky," look at some racing shoes. After you have broken them in, you can use the lighter shoes during speed sessions.

A watch

There are a lot of good, inexpensive watches which will give you accurate times on your speed workouts and races. Any watch that has a stopwatch function will do the job. Be sure to ask the staff person in the store how to use the stopwatch. A few watches can make walk breaks easier by "beeping" after each running segment and then again after the walking segment.

For more information on current watches that do this, go to *www.RunInjuryFree.com*.

Clothing: comfort above all

The "clothing thermometer" at the end of this book is a great guide for this area. In the summer, you want to wear light, cool clothing. During cold weather, layers are the best strategy. You don't have to have the

latest techno-garments to run. On most days an old pair of shorts and a T-shirt are fine. As you get into the various components of your plan, you will find various outfits that make you feel better and motivate you to get in your run even on bad weather days. It is also OK to give yourself a fashionable outfit as a "reward" for running regularly for several weeks.

A training journal

The journal is such an important component in running that I have written a chapter about it. By using it to plan ahead and then later, to review mistakes, you take a major degree of control over your running future. You'll find it reinforcing to write down what you did each day, and miss that reinforcement when you skip. Be sure to read the training journal chapter, and you too, can take control over your running future.

Where to run

It helps to have several different venues for the various workouts. Try to find 2 or more options for each:

Long runs   — scenic, interesting areas are best—with some pavement and some softer surface if possible

Pace work   — a track or any accurately measured segment

Races & Tests — Look carefully at the course—avoid hills, too many turns, or even too much flat terrain if you usually train on rolling hills (in a non-hilly race, you will fatigue your flat running muscles more quickly, if you don't run long runs on flat terrain). Read the section on racing.

| Drills | — any safe running area with a secure surface |

Safety—top priority!

Pick a course that is away from car traffic, and is in a safe area—where crime is unlikely. Try to have 2 or more options for each of the components because variety can be very motivating.

Convenience

If you have an option near home and office, for each of the training components listed above, you will be more likely to do the workouts on your schedule—when you need to do them.

Surface

With the correct amount of cushion, and the selection of the right shoes for you, pavement should not give extra shock to the legs or body. A smooth surface dirt or gravel path, is a preferred surface for the easy days.

But beware of an uneven surface especially if you have weak ankles or foot problems. For your tests, speedwork, and drills, you may have to talk to your shoe experts to avoid blisters, etc. when running on certain types of surfaces. Watch the slant of the road, trail, track or sidewalk—flat is best.

Picking a running companion

On long runs and on easy days, don't run with someone who is faster than you—unless they are fully comfortable slowing down to an easy pace—that is...slow for you. It is motivating to run with someone who will go slowly enough so that you can talk. Share stories, jokes, problems if you wish, and you'll bond together in a very positive way.

The friendships forged on runs can be the strongest and longest lasting—if you're not huffing and puffing (or puking) from trying to run at a pace that is too fast. On speed days, however, it sometimes helps to run with a faster person as long as you are running at the pace you should be running in each workout.

Rewards

You'll see in the section on "setting yourself up for running success" that rewards are important at all times. Be sensitive and provide rewards that will keep you motivated, and make the running experience a better one (more comfortable shoes, clothes, etc.).

Positive reinforcement works! Treating yourself to a smoothie after a hard run, taking a cool dip in a pool, going out to a special restaurant after a longer run—all of these can reinforce the successful completion of another week or month. Of particular benefit is having a snack, within 30 minutes of the finish of a run, that has about 200-300 calories, containing 80% carbohydrate and 20% protein.

The products Accelerade and Endurox R4 are already formulated with this ratio for your convenience, and give you a recovery boost also.

An appointment on the calendar

Write down each of your weekly runs, transposed from your 52 week plan, at least 2 weeks in advance, on your calendar or journal. Since each week is broken down for you in this book, you can use it as your guide. Sure you can change if you have to. But by having a secure running slot, you will be able to plan for your run, and make it happen. Pretend that this is an appointment with your boss, or your most important client, etc. Actually, you are your most important client!

Motivation to get out the door

There are two times when runners feel challenged to run: early in the morning and after work, or before the tough workouts. In the motivation section there are rehearsals for each of these situations. You will find it much easier to be motivated once you experience a regular series of runs that make you feel good. Yes, when you run and walk at the right pace, with the right preparation, you feel better, can relate to others better, and have more energy to enjoy the rest of the day.

Treadmills are just as good as streets for short runs

More and more runners are using treadmills for at least 50% of their runs—particularly those who have small children. It is a fact that treadmills tend to tell you that you have gone further or faster than you really have (but usually are not off by more than 10%). But if you run on a treadmill for the number of minutes assigned, at the effort level you are used to (no huffing and puffing), you will get close enough to the training effect you wish. To ensure that you have run enough miles, feel free to add 10% to your assigned mileage.

Usually no need to eat before the run

Most runners don't need to eat before runs that are less than 6 miles. The only exceptions are those with diabetes or severe blood sugar problems. Many runners feel better during a run when they have enjoyed a cup of coffee about an hour before the start. Caffeine engages the central nervous system, which gets all of the systems needed for exercise up and running to capacity, very quickly.

If your blood sugar is low, which often occurs in the afternoon, it helps to have a snack of about 100-200 calories, about 30 minutes before the run, that is composed of 80% carbohydrate and 20% protein. The Accelerade product has been very successful.

Heart disease and running

Running tends to have a protective effect from cardiovascular disease. But more runners die of heart disease than any other cause, and are susceptible to the same risk factors as sedentary people. Like most other citizens, runners at risk usually don't know that they are. I know of a number of runners who have suffered heart attacks and strokes who probably could have prevented them if they had taken a few simple tests. Some of these are listed below, but check with your doctor if you have any questions or concerns.

Your heart is the most important organ in your body. This short section is offered as a guide to help you take charge over your cardiovascular health to maintain a high level of fitness in the most important organ for longevity, and quality of life. As always, you need to get advice about your individual situation from a cardiologist who knows you and specializes in this area.

Risk factors—get checked if you have two of these—or one that is serious

- Family history
- Poor lifestyle habits earlier in life
- High fat/high cholesterol diet
- Have smoked—or still smoke
- Obese or severely overweight
- High blood pressure
- High cholesterol

Tests

- Stress test—heart is monitored during a run that gradually increases in difficulty
- C reactive protein—has been an indicator of increased risk
- Heart scan—an electronic scan of the heart which shows calcification, and possible narrowing of arteries
- Radioactive dye test—very effective in locating specific blockages. Talk to your doctor about this.
- Carotid ultrasound test—helps to tell if you're at risk for stroke
- Ankle-brachial test—plaque build-up in arteries throughout the body

None of these are foolproof. But by working with your cardiologist, you can increase your chance of living until the muscles just won't propel you further down the road—past the age of 100.

Should I run when I have a cold?

There are so many individual health issues with a cold that you must talk with a doctor before you exercise when you have an infection.

Lung infection—don't run! A virus in the lungs can move into the heart and kill you. Lung infections are usually indicated by coughing.

Common cold? There are many infections that initially indicate a normal cold but are not—they may be much more serious. At least call your doctor's office to get clearance before running. Be sure to explain how much you are running, and what, if any medication you are taking.

Infections of the throat and above the neck—most runners will be given the OK, but check with the doc.

Risk of speed

There is an increased risk of both injuries and cardiovascular events during speed sessions. Be sure to get your doctor's OK before beginning a speed program. The advice inside this book is generally conservative, but when in doubt, take more rest, more days off, and run slower. In other words...be more conservative.

BUILDING A CONDITIONING BASE FOR PERFORMANCE

When you look carefully at the 52 week plan, you'll see several stages of training, which I compare to a pyramid. The first few weeks are mostly slow running, focusing on a gradual increase in the length of a slow long run. As you continue to increase endurance through the long one, you'll add hills for leg strength. The hill repeats should be a gentle introduction to faster running, preparing the legs and body for the speedwork that will come. In other words, hill repeats provide a great transition between slow running of the first few weeks, and the more intense speed repetition workouts, later in the program.

But you'll also see that diverse elements are woven together throughout the year so that you continue to improve speed, and endurance. The whole process is like a symphony of elements, that blend mind and body, heart and legs, left brain and right into an integrated success.

Our bodies are designed to improve through a series of challenges

I believe that distance running engages the various systems in our bodies that connect us directly to our roots. Primitive man had to walk and run for survival—thousands of miles a year. Through millions of years of evolution, the muscles, tendons, bones, energy systems, cardiovascular capacity adapted and expanded. Over this extended period, a series of psychological rewards developed. This is why we feel good when we run and walk at the correct (conservative) pace for us.

The "Team" of heart, lungs, nerves, brain, etc.

Very often, in college and professional sports, a group of very talented individuals is defeated by a solid team of players with lesser ability. In a similar way, running helps to mold your key body organs into a coordinated unit. When running within one's capacity, the right brain uses its intuitive and creative powers to solve problems, manage resources, and help us find the pace and amount of training that we can handle. While the heart is our primary blood pump, your leg muscles, when fit, will provide significant help in pushing blood back to the heart.

The heart gets stronger—like any muscle, the heart's strength and effectiveness is increased through regular endurance exercise.

The lungs—become more efficient in processing oxygen and inserting it into the blood

Endorphins (natural painkillers) reduce discomfort, and give you a relaxing and positive attitude

The long run builds endurance By gradually extending slow long runs, you train muscle cells to expand their capacity to utilize oxygen efficiently, sustain energy production, and in general, increase capacity to go farther. The continued increase of the distance of long runs increases the reach of blood artery capillaries to deliver oxygen and improves the return of waste products so that the muscles can work at top capacity. In short, long runs bestow a better plumbing system, improving muscle capacity. These changes will pay off when you do speed training.

Even when running very slowly, with liberal walk breaks, you build endurance by gradually increasing the distance of a regularly scheduled long run. Start with the length of your current long one, and increase by 0.5 to 1 mile per week, as noted in the following schedule:

- With a current long run of 1-2 miles, increase by half a mile each week
- When the long run reaches 4-6 miles you can increase by one mile each week
- When the long run exceeds 9 miles, you can increase by 1-2 miles every 2 weeks, running half that amount on the non long run weekend
- When the long run exceeds 17 miles, you can increase by 2-3 miles every 3 weeks, running 7-9 miles on the non long run weekend

Maintain current endurance by running two 30 minute runs, every other day (i.e., Tues and Thurs)

A half hour run on Tuesday and Thursday will maintain the endurance gained on the weekend. This is the minimum and results in the lowest injury rate. If you are already running more than this, without aches and pains, you can continue if you wish. As you will see in the 52 week plan, more training is needed to achieve most of the time goals.

To summarize, the long runs on weekends, with two other runs during the week will create a level of fitness and muscle strength sufficient for starting a speed training program. At the same time, you'll be improving the internal engineering of the muscles: enhanced oxygen absorption, increased blood flow, better energy supply and storage, and much more. Speedwork improves the mechanical efficiency of the bones, muscles, tendons, as they adapt and you become more efficient as a runner.

HILL TRAINING BUILDS STRENGTH —AND MORE

Hill training strengthens the legs for running, better than any other activity I know. At the same time it can help you maximize your stride length, increase leg speed, and improve your ability to run hills in races. The hill training period provides a gentle introduction to faster running, while improving your capacity to perform the speedwork later in the program.

You'll see on the 52 week plan that hills are gradually introduced into the program, while the long runs are increasing. Complete rest (by walking down the hill) is recommended after each hill so that injury risk is reduced to a very low level. A day off from running is also recommended after running hills.

The hill workout

- Walk for 5 minutes.
- Jog and walk to a hill—about 10 minutes. Jog a minute and walk a minute (a longer warm-up is fine).
- Do 4 acceleration-gliders. These are listed in the "Drills" chapter (don't sprint).
- Reverse this warm-up as your warm down.
- Choose a hill with a gentle grade—steep hills often cause problems and bestow no benefit.
- Walk to the top of the hill. Then step off the length of your hill segment by walking down from the top:

50	walking steps for beginners

100-150	steps for those who have done a little speed work before

| 150-200 | steps for those who have done speedwork, but not within the past 6 months |

| 200-300 | steps for those who have been doing regular speedwork |

- Mark the place after you step it off. This is where each hill starts. Walk to the bottom of the hill.
- Run up the hill for 5 seconds, and then down for 5 seconds. Walk for 30-60 seconds. Repeat this 5-10 times. This finalizes the warm-up.
- Walk for 3-4 minutes.
- Run the first few steps of each hill acceleration at a jog, then gradually pick up the turnover of the feet as you go up the hill.
- Get into a comfortable rhythm, so that you can gradually increase this rhythm or turnover (# of RPM's of feet and legs) as you go up the hill.
- Keep stride length short—and keep shortening stride as you go up the hill.
- It's OK to huff and puff at the top of the hill—but don't let the legs get over extended, or feel exhausted.
- Run over the top of the hill by at least 10 steps.
- Jog back to the top of the hill and walk down to recover between the hills. Walk as much as you need for complete recovery after each hill.

Hill running form

- Start with a comfortable stride—fairly short.
- As you go up the hill, shorten the stride.
- Touch lightly with your feet.
- Maintain a body posture that is perpendicular to the horizontal (upright, not leaning forward or back).

- Pick up the turnover of your feet as you go up and over the top.

- Keep adjusting stride so that the leg muscles don't tighten up—you want them as resilient as possible.

- Relax as you go over the top of the hill, and glide (or coast) a bit on the downside.

Hill training strengthens lower legs and improves running form

The incline of the hill forces your legs to work harder as you go up. The extra work up the incline and the faster turnover, builds strength. By taking an easy walk between the hills, and an easy day afterward, the lower leg muscles become stronger. Over several months, the improved strength allows you to support your body weight farther forward on your feet. An extended range of motion of the ankle and achilles tendon results in a "bonus" extension of the foot forward— with no increase in effort. You will run faster without working harder. What a deal!

Running faster on hills in races

Once you train yourself to run with efficient hill form, you'll run faster with increased turnover on the hill workouts. This prepares you to do the same in races. You won't run quite as fast in a race as in your workouts. But through hill training you can run faster than you used to run up the same hill on a race course.

Race hill technique is the same as in workouts: keep shortening stride as you move up the hill. Monitor your respiration rate: don't huff and puff more than you were doing on the flat. As runners improve their hill technique in races, they find that a shorter and quicker stride reduces effort while increasing speed—with no increase in breathing.

Downhill form

- Run light on your feet.
- Maintain an average stride.
- Keep feet low to the ground.
- Let gravity pull you down the hill.
- Turnover of the feet will pick up.
- Try to glide (or coast) quickly down the hill.

Biggest mistakes: too long a stride, bouncing too much

Even when your stride is one or two inches too long, your downhill speed can get out of control. If you are bouncing more than an inch or two off the ground you run the risk of pounding your feet, having to use your quads to slow down (producing soreness) and creating hamstring soreness due to overstride. Best indicator of overstride is having tight hamstrings (big muscle behind your upper leg).

Note:
On your long runs and easy running days, just jog up hills, don't run faster up the hill. If your breathing is increasing on a hill, reduce effort and stride length until your respiration is as it was on the flat ground.

SPEED TRAINING PREPARES YOU FOR TOP PERFORMANCE

Getting faster requires extra work

To get faster, you must push beyond your current performance capacity. But you must be careful. Even a small amount over your speed limit, can result in longer recovery or injury. The secret is to push only a little harder on each workout, then back off so the systems can rebound and improve. Gradual and gentle increases are always better because you are more likely to sustain a continuous and long-term improvement.

Our bodies are programmed to conserve resources by doing the smallest amount of work they can get away with. So even after we have increased the length of our runs, steadily over several months, our leg muscles, tendons, ligaments etc., are not prepared for the jolt that speed training delivers. The best way to stay injury-free is to gradually increase the duration and intensity. But only when we put the legs, the heart, the lungs, etc., to a gentle test, week by week, does the body respond by improving in dozens of ways.

- Mitochondria (energy powerhouse inside muscle cell) increase capacity and output

- Mechanical efficiency of the foot is improved—more work with less effort

- Legs go further when tired—adaptations allow you to keep going

- Muscle cells work as a team—getting stronger, increasing performance, pumping blood back to heart.

- Mental concentration increases

- Your spirit is unleashed as you find yourself improving

Endorphins kill pain, make you feel good

Running at any pace, but especially speed training, signals to your body that there will be some pain to kill. The natural response is to produce natural pain killers called endorphins. These hormones act as drugs that relax and deal with muscle discomfort, while bestowing a good attitude—especially when you are tired after the run. Walking during the rest interval allows the endorphins to collect.

Gradually pushing up the workload

Your body is programmed to improve, when it is gradually introduced to a little more work, with enough rest afterward. Push too hard, or neglect the rest, and you'll see an increase in aches, pains, and injury. When speed workouts are balanced, adjustments are made to legitimate problems, and goals are realistic, most runners can continue to improve for years.

Stress + Rest = Improvement

When we run a little faster than our realistic goal pace, and increase the the number of repetitions a little more than we did on last week's speed workout, this greater workload slightly breaks down the muscle cells, tendons, etc. just enough to stimulate change. You see, our bodies are programmed to rebuild, stronger than before when slightly overwhelmed. But there must be gentle and regular stress, followed by significant rest to promote this regeneration.

Introducing the body to speed through "drills"

As a gentle introduction to faster running, I've found nothing better than the two drills that are detailed in the

"Drills" chapter: Turnover Drills & Acceleration-Gliders. The former helps to improve cadence of the legs and feet. The latter provides a very gentle introduction to speedwork, in very short segments. Most of the running during the conditioning period is at an easy pace. These drills, done in the middle of a short run, once or twice a week, will improve mechanics, get the muscles ready for the heavier demands of speed training, and initiate internal physiological changes in the muscles—with very little risk of injury.

A gentle increase in your weekly workouts causes a slight breakdown

The weekly speed workout starts with a few speed repetitions, with rest between each. As the number of repetitions increase each week your body is pushed slightly beyond what it did the previous week. In each workout, your muscle fibers get tired as they reach the previous maximum workload, and continue like motivated slaves to keep you running the pace assigned.

In every session some are pushed beyond their capacity with each additional speed repetition. Often, pain and fatigue are not felt during the workout. But within one or two days there are usually sore muscles and tendons, and general overall tiredness. Even walking may not feel smooth for a day or two after a speed session that is run too hard.

The damage

Looking inside the cell at the end of a hard workout, you'll see damage:

- Tears in the muscle cell membrane.
- The mitochondria (that process the energy inside the cell) are swollen.
- There's a significant lowering of the muscle stores of glycogen (the energy supply needed in speedwork).
- Waste products from exertion, bits of bone and muscle tissue and other bio junk can be found.
- Sometimes, there are small tears in the blood vessels and arteries, and blood leaks into the muscles.

The damage stimulates the muscles, tendons, etc to rebuild stronger and better than before

Your body is programmed to get better when it is pushed beyond its current limits. A slight increase is better than a greater increase because the repair can be done relatively quickly.

You must have enough rest—if you want to rebuild stronger and better

Two days after a speed session, if the muscles have had enough rest, you'll see some improvements:
- Waste has been removed.
- Thicker cell membranes can handle more work without breaking down.
- The mitochondria have increased in size and number, so that they can process more energy next time.
- The damage to the blood system has been repaired.
- Over several months, after adapting to a continued series of small increases, more capillaries (tiny fingers of the blood system) are produced. This improves and expands the delivery of oxygen and nutrients and provides a better withdrawal of waste products.

These are only some of the many adaptations made by the incredible human body, when we exercise: bio-mechanics, nervous system, strength, muscle efficiency and more. Internal psychological improvements follow the physical ones. Mind, body, and spirit are becoming a team, improving health and performance. An added benefit is a positive attitude.

Quality rest is crucial: 48 hours between workouts

On rest days, it's important to avoid exercises that strenuously use the calf muscle, ankle and achilles tendon (stair machines, step aerobics, spinning out of the saddle) for the 48 hour period between running workouts. If you have other aches and pains from your individual "weak links" then don't do exercises that aggravate them further. Walking is usually a great exercise for a rest day. There are several other good exercises in the "Cross Training" section of this book. As long as you are not continuing to stress the calf, most alternative exercises are fine.

Beware of junk miles

Those training for a time goal often develop injuries because they try to "sneak in" a few miles on the days they should be resting. Even more than running long distance, speed training stresses the feet and legs and mandates the need for a 48 hour recovery period. The short, junk mile days don't help your conditioning, but they keep your muscles from recovering.

Regularity

To maintain the adaptations, you must regularly run, about every 2 days. To maintain the speed improvements mentioned in this book, you should do the speed work listed in the training scheduled, about every week. It is OK to delay a workout every once in a while, but you need to stay on the schedule as close as possible. Missing two workouts in a row, will result in a slight loss in the capacity you have been developing. The longer you wait, the harder it will be to start up again.

"Muscle memory"

Your neuro-muscular system remembers the patterns of muscle activity which you have done regularly, over an extended period of time. The longer you have been running regularly, the more easily it will be to start up when you've had a layoff. During your first few months of speedwork, for example, if you miss a weekly workout, you will need to drop back a week, and rebuild. But if you have run regularly for several years, and you miss a speed workout, little will be lost if you start the next one very slowly, and ease into it. Be careful as you return to speed training, if this happens.

Tip: Cramped for time? Just do a few repetitions

Let's say that you cannot get to the track on your speed day, and you don't have but 15 minutes to run. Take a 3-4 minute slow warm-up with some accelerations, and do the same, in reverse, during the last 3-5 minutes. During the middle 5-9 minutes, run several 1-2 minute accelerations at approximately the pace you would run on the track. Don't worry if the pace is not perfect. Doing any of these segments is better than a week without any fast running at all. Then, the following week, you can do the workout (or most of it)that had been planned this week.

Aerobic running is done during long runs

Aerobic means "in the presence of oxygen." This is the type of running you do when you feel "slow" and comfortable. When running aerobically, your muscles can get enough oxygen from the blood to process the energy in the cells (burning fat in most cases). The minimal waste products produced during aerobic running can be easily removed, with no lingering build-up in the muscles.

Speed training gets you into the anaerobic zone: an oxygen debt

Anaerobic running means running too fast or too long for you, on that day. At some point in the workout, when you reach your current limit, the muscles can't get enough oxygen to burn the most efficient fuel, fat. So they shift to the limited supply of stored sugar: glycogen. The waste products from this fuel pile up quickly in the cells, tightening the muscles and causing you to breathe heavily. This is called an oxygen debt. If you keep running for too long in this anaerobic state, you will have to slow down significantly or stop. But if you are running for a realistic time goal, and are pacing yourself correctly, you should only be running anaerobically for a short period of time, at the end of each workout and race.

The anaerobic threshold

As you increase the quantity of your speed sessions, you push back your anaerobic threshold. This means that you can run a bit farther than before—each week, at the same pace, without extreme huffing and puffing. Your muscles can move your body farther and faster without going to exhaustion. Each speed workout pushes you a little bit further into the anaerobic zone. Testing yourself means running with an oxygen debt. Speed training teaches the body and mind that they can go farther before going anaerobic, how to deal with the discomfort this produces, and how to keep going when the muscles are tight and tired. It also tells you that you don't have to give up on performance when in this state. The process of coping with the stress of speedwork is the essence of running faster.

The talk test—how aerobic are you?

- You're aerobic—if you can talk for as long as you want with minimal huffing & puffing(h & p)
- You are mostly aerobic—if you can talk for 30 sec + then must h & p for no more than 10 sec
- You are approaching anaerobic threshold—if you can only talk for 10 seconds or less, then h & p for 10 + sec
- You're anaerobic—if you can't talk more than a few words, and are mostly huffing and puffing

Fast twitch vs. slow twitch muscle fibers

We are born with a combination of two types of muscle fibers. Those with a high percentage of fast twitchers can run fast for a short distance, and then become very tired. Fast twitch fibers are designed to burn the stored sugar in your muscles: glycogen. This is the fuel we use during the first 15 minutes of exercise (and during speedwork), and it can produce a lot of waste product, such as lactic acid. If we run even a little too fast at the beginning of a run, the muscles will become very tight and tired, very quickly, you will huff and puff, and feel increasingly uncomfortable.

If you have more slow twitch fibers, you won't be able to run as fast at first, but can keep going for longer distances. Slow twitch fibers burn fat—a fuel that is very efficient and produces little waste product. Long runs will not only condition the slow twitch fibers to work to top capacity as they efficiently burn fat. As you increase the length of the long ones, you'll train some of your fast twitch fibers to burn fat as fuel—and function as slow twitchers.

Once the starting pace is controlled (and also the ego), fast runners develop a mix of fast and slow twitchers to do the work of running, and find that they don't get exhausted at the end. It is the slow pace and walk breaks that keep you in the aerobic (or fat-burning)zone, allowing you to push back the endurance limit.

Are you working too hard toward a time goal?

When runners get too focused on specific time goals they often feel more stress and experience some negative attitude changes. At the first sign of these symptoms, back off and let mind and body get back together again.

- Running is not as enjoyable

- You don't look forward to your runs

- When you say something to others about your running, the statements are often negative

- The negativity can permeate other areas of your life

- You look on running as work instead of play

The personal growth of speed training

Instead of looking just at the times in your races, embrace the life lessons that can come from the journey of an extended speed training program. Most of your runs must have some fun in them, to help you through the challenges. Even after a hard workout, focus on how good you feel afterward, and the satisfaction from overcoming the adversity.

Note:
There's more on this topic in the Mental Toughness chapter.

The reality of a speed training program is that you'll have more setbacks than victories. But you will learn more from the setbacks and they will make you a stronger runner—and a stronger person. Confronting challenges is initially tough, but leads you to some of the great treasure of the improvement process. As you dig for deeper resources you find that you have more strength inside than you thought—as you discover the path to solutions that initally seemed to be too challenging for that day.

HOW SPEED
TRAINING
WORKS

Marathon runners have known for decades that training for a shorter race will get the racing systems ready to run faster in the longer event. The 52 week schedule will prepare you for a series of races, leading to a marathon. The faster pace of both the workouts and the 5K, 10K races themselves, force the muscles, tendons, nerves, cardiovascular system, psyche, and spirit to gear up.

The regularity of the workouts set up a process that improves efficiency. You'll also search for and find new resources needed to deal with the challenges not faced before. For example, once you have trained to run faster, at the 10K distance, the pace for a marathon or half marathon seems easier. You also tend to feel smoother when running this longer distance.

Fact: running faster at a shorter distance can improve longer distance times

- To run a faster Marathon, train to run a faster Half Marathon
- To run a faster half marathon, train to run a faster 10K
- To run a faster 10K, train to run a faster 5K
- To run a faster 5K, train to run a faster mile

Training for the faster race stresses the systems to improve Each week, as you add slightly to the amount done in your speed workout, you slightly overwhelm the muscles and cardiovascular system. Your body has the incredible capacity to respond to this challenge by rebuilding stronger than before, with better efficiency.

The faster speedwork develops systems that perform at a higher capacity

The faster pace of your speed workout coaxes adaptations out of the tendons, muscles, nerve system, leg and foot mechanics. You touch lighter, use your ankle and leg muscles more efficiently, while building the strength and internal physiology to run faster.

Sustained speed—through an increase in the number of repetitions

The maximum benefit from speed sessions, is at the end of the program. As you increase the number of speed repetitions from 4 to 6, 8 and beyond, you teach yourself how to keep going at your assigned pace, even when tired. To maintain speed when tired—is the mission. The only way to prepare for this "race reality" situation is to do this during speed training. Speedwork teaches you and your legs that they con keep performing even when very tired. The result is that you won't slow down as you would before speedwork.

Longer runs maintain endurance—and improve your time

Your long runs will maintain or extend endurance, while you improve speed. Every week or two you'll run a very slow longer run. Many runners improve their times through this long run increase as much as or more than from speed training. Both are important for maximum improvement.

Running form improves

Regular speed workouts stimulate your body to run more efficiently. On each workout, as you push into fatigue, your body intuitively searches for ways of continuing to move at the same pace without extraneous motion: lighter touch of the feet, direct foot lift, lower to the ground, quicker turnover. See the running form chapter for more details.

Watch out! Speedwork increases aches, pains and injuries

Be sensitive to the areas on your foot, leg, muscles, etc., where you've had problems before—your weak links. Think back to the patterns of aches and pains that have caused you to reduce or stop exercise in the past. You can reduce injury risk significantly by taking a day of two off at the flare-up of one of these, and by following the tips in the "aches and pains" chapter in this book.

PRIME
TRAINING
ELEMENTS

In the 52 week plan you will be presented with workouts that help to develop specific capabilities. They are like components in a sound system, which, when blended together create a wonderful sound that is greater than the sum of its parts. Please don't try to combine two or more of these—unless they are listed that way on the schedule. For example, you can do acceleration-gliders and cadence drills as a warm-up before speed or hill sessions. But if you try to accelerate in any way, during a long run, you will increase recovery time, and may injure yourself.

Long runs—Run these very slowly—at least 2 min/mi slower than you could run in a marathon as predicted by your one mile test. Put in the walk breaks that are suggested in the Run-Walk-Run tm chapter in this book. You cannot go too slow on long runs. Slower long runs build the same endurance as fast long runs—with little or no risk of injury or burnout.

Drills—Cadence Drills (CD) and Acceleration Gliders (Acg). These easy exercises teach your body to improve form, as you improve running mechanics. They are not exhausting— most runners say they energize an average run. Doing each of these drills, once a week, will improve speed and running efficiency.

Test races—These are done every few weeks to monitor progress, and overtraining.

- Go to a track, or other accurately measured course.
- Warm up by walking for 5 minutes, then running a minute and walking a minute, then jogging an easy 800 meter (half mile or two laps around a track).
- Do 4 acceleration-gliders. These are listed in the "Drills" chapter.

- Walk for 3-4 minutes.
- Run the 1 mile test (or 5K)—a hard effort. Follow the walk break suggestions in the "Predicting Performance" chapter.
- On your first race, don't run all-out from the start—ease into your pace after the first third of the distance.
- Warm down by reversing the warm-up.
- A school track is the best venue. Don't use a treadmill because they tend to be notoriously un-calibrated, and often tell you that you ran farther or faster than you really did. Run the first lap slightly slower than you think you can average. Take a short walk break as noted in the walk break suggestions in this chapter. It is OK to be huffing and puffing on the last lap. If you are slowing down on the last lap, start a little slower on the next test. When you finish, you should feel like you couldn't run more than about half a lap further at that pace (if that).

Speed (s)—A gradual increase in speed training can prepare you for the realistic goal of your choice. See the speedwork section of this book.

Pace (p)—On these runs, you want to run at race pace, taking the walk breaks as you plan to take them in the race. This is like a dress rehearsal for race day. By doing this exactly as you plan to do in your race, you will be ready.

- Warm up with 5 min of walking, then 10 min of easy running and walking.
- Time yourself for a segment that is between half a mile and 2 miles
- Run at your goal pace
- Insert walk breaks as you plan to do so in the race

- Do 1-3 miles of these segments
- Don't do them if your legs are too tired
- Reverse the warm up as a warm down

Track distances

800m is approximately half a mile, or two laps around a track.
1 mi is one mile, or 4 laps around a track.

Goal races

These are printed on the 52 week plan in bold print. In each phase of training, there is a goal race: 5K, 10K, half marathon, marathon. You may choose to run these hard, or just run through them. It is possible to set personal records in all of the goal races in a year, but this is rare.

Secondary races

There are several slots on the calendar for secondary races. These give you a chance to see where you are, performance wise. Try to have fun in all of your races—but particularly the secondary ones.

THE 52
WEEK PLAN

Note:
There's more
on this topic
in the Mental
Toughness
chapter.

Included here is a yearly cycle. You will decide when your major goal of the year will be run. It accounts for periods when the legs, body and mind can back off a bit, in order to rebound. While it is structured, each person will need to modify it according to the "life events" that we all experience.

These schedules assume that you have been running (with appropriate walk breaks) the amount listed in the first week of the schedule without struggling. If you have not, then gradually build up to this amount before beginning the program. If you are doing more than is noted on the schedule, you can continue with the greater amount as long as you are not having trouble recovering from this amount. When in doubt, cut back to the amount on the schedule.

XT—means "cross training" Any exercise that does not use the calf muscle is usually fine. Excluded exercises are stair machines, spinning on the bicycle when standing on the pedals, and step aerobics. Water running is best, and improves running. In some cases I have included the amount of cross training for a given day.

This is optional. Cross training is mainly helpful in giving the "type A" running personalities some exercise on a day that should not be a running day. Water running is the only XT exercise I believe can improve running. Be sure to read about it in the appropriate section in this book, or in *Galloway's Book On Running, 2nd Edition*.

Three schedules:

"A" Schedule — for runners who have never raced, who have no time goal—but who are going to finish.

"B" Schedule — for runners who want to do a few races a year, and want to improve a little (1-3%)

"C" Schedule — for runners who have raced the goal distance, and want to improve to max potential (4-5%)

- The weeks are numbered, so that you can simply start whenever your want. I suggest that you count back from your major goal race.

- Please, don't run any speedwork or races during the 3 weeks after the marathon, and during the 2 weeks after a half marathon.

- Don't run test races, hill workouts, or speed sessions if you sense that the legs are injured or significantly tired from the previous week's workouts.

- Be very careful running the hills or speed sessions if the legs are still tired from the last workout.

- CD means "cadence drill" These are usually done on Tues after an easy mile. See chapter on Drills for instructions.

- Acg means "acceleration-glider" These are usually done on Tues after the CD. See chapter on Drills for instructions

- Pace (p) means "pace segments". During a Thurs run, run at the goal pace of the next race (taking walk breaks) This is a "dress rehearsal" for the race itself.

- Hills refer to hill repeats—see previous section for description of workout—this is a Thursday workout

- Speed (s) refers to the speed workout for that week:

  (m-s)   One mile repeats for the marathon, 30 sec faster than goal pace, walking 5 min between each

  (h-s)   800 meter repeats for half marathon, 15 sec/800 faster than goal pace, walk 3min between each

  (10/5K-s) 400 meter repeats for 10K or shorter, 5-7 sec faster than goal pace, walk 2 min between each

- The last few weeks of each program are designed for recovering, and letting the body heal any damage that has accumulated over the past year or so. You won't lose any conditioning by reducing your running and going slowly during this period. This will let the legs "freshen up" for the next 52 weeks.

- If you need to delay a goal race, simply put an easy week or two into the program. If you have a month of delay, you can either start later, or repeat the 4 weeks leading up to the goal race.

"A" Plan (Tues)				Key Weekend Run	
Week#	CD	Acg	Pace(p)/ Speed(s)	Hills	or Race Speed or Long or Run or Race
1.	2	0		0	1mi
2.	3	2		0	1.5mi
3.	4	3		0	2mi
4.	4	4		1	2.5mi
5.	4	4		2	3mi
6.	4	4		2	3.5mi
7.	4	4		2	3 mi (including 1 mi test)
8.	4	4		3	4.0mi
9.	4	4		3	4.5mi
10.	4	4		3	3 mi(including 1mi test)
11.	4	4		3	5mi
12.	4	4		4	5.5 mi
13.	4	4		2-3	5K race
14.	4	4		2	6 mi easy
15.	4	4		4	2 mi easy
16.	4	4		2	7 mi
17.	4	4		3-4	1 mi test (3mi total)
18.	4	4		0	8 mi very slow
19.	4	4		0	10K race
20.	4	4		3	3 mi
21.	4	4		0	7.5 mi
22.	4	4		3-4	3 mi
23.	4	4		0	9 mi
24.	4	4		3-4	3 mi
25.	4	4		0	10.5 mi
26.	4	4		2	1 mi test (3 mi total)
27.	4	4		0	12 mi
28.	4	4		3-4	3 mi
29.	4	4		0	13.5 mi
30.	4	4		3-4	3 mi

31.	4	4	0		15 mi
32.	4	4	3-4		1 mi test, 3 mi total
33.	4	4	0		Half Marathon Race
34.	4	4	2		3 mi
35.	4	4	0		16-17
36.	4	4	2		3-4 mi
37.	4	4	0		18-19 mi
38.	4	4	2		3-4 mi
39.	4	4	2		1 mile test (5 mi total)
40.	4	4	0		20-21 mi
41.	4	4	2		4-5 mi
42.	4	4	2		1 mi test (6 mi total)
43.	4	4	0		22-23 miles
44.	4	4	2		4-6 miles
45.	4	4	2		1 mi test (7 mi total)
46.	4	4	0		24-26 miles
47.	4	4	0		4-6 miles
48.	4	4	2	scenic run	1 mi test (7 mi total)
49.	4	4	0		Marathon Goal Race
50.	0	0	0		4-6 mi
51.	2	2	1	social	6-8 mi
52.	4	4	2		6-12 mi

"B" Plan (Tues)				Key Weekend Run	
Week#	CD	Acg	Pace(p)/Speed(s)	Hills	Speed or Long Run or Race
1.	2	2		1	2mi
2.	3	3		2	3mi
3.	4	4		3	4mi
4.	5	5		4	5mi
5.	6	6		5	6mi(with 1mile test)
6.	7	7		6	7mi
7.	8	8		7	8mi
8.	8	8	4x400(10Ks)	6	4mi(with 1mi test)

9.	6	6	6x400(10Ks)	4	9mi
10.	6	6	8x400(10Ks)	4	5K race + 2mi easy
11.	4	4	10x400(10Ks)	4	10mi
12.	4	4	12x400(10Ks)	2	5K race plus 2 mi easy
13.	4	4	14x400(10Ks)	1	12 mi
14.	4	4	16x400(10Ks)	0	1 mi test (5mi total)
15.	4	4	18x400(10Ks)	0	14 mi
16.	4	4	20x400(10Ks)	0	3 x800 (half-s)
17.	4	4		2-3	16 mi
18.	4	4	4x400(10Kp)	2	5-6x800 (half-s)
19.	4	4	4x400(10Kp)	2	10K Goal Race
20.	4	4		0	18 mi
21.	4	4	2x800(Half-p)	2	7-9x800(half-s)
22.	4	4	3x800(Half-p)	0	9-11x800(half-s)
23.	4	4	2x800(Half-p)	0	19-20 mi
24.	4	4		0	11-13x800(half-s)
25.	4	4	3x400(5K speed)	2	1 mile test (5 mi total)
26.	4	4	5x400(5K speed)	2	Half Marathon Goal
27.	4	4		0	4 mi—EASY WEEK
28.	4	4	7x400(5K speed)	2	
29.	4	4	9x400(5K speed)	2	1 mi test (5 mi total)
30.	4	4	11X400(5K speed)	2	17 miles
31.	4	4	13x400(5K speed)	2	4x1mile (m-s)
32.	4	4	3x1mile(m-p)	2	5K Goal Race
33.	4	4		0	20 miles
34.	4	4	3x1mile(m-p)	2	6 x 1 mile (m-s)
35.	4	4	3x1mile(m-p)	2	8x1mi (m-s)
36.	4	4		0	23 miles
37.	4	4	3x1mile(m-p)	2	10x1mi (m-s)
38.	4	4	2x1mile(m-p)	2	1 mile test (6 mi total)
39.	4	4		0	26 miles
40.	4	4	2x1mile(m-p)	2	8 mi easy
41.	4	4	2x1mile(m-p)	2	12 x 1 mi (m-s)
42.	4	4	2x1mile(m-p)	2	1 mile test (8 mi total)

Week#	CD	Acg	Pace(p)/Speed(s)	Hills	Speed or Long Run or Race
43.	4	4	1x 1mile(m-p)	0	29 miles
44.	4	4	2x1mi (m-p)	2	4 x 1 mi
45.	4	4	2x1mi (m-p)	2	13 x 1 mile (m-s)
46.	4	4	2x1mi(m-p)	2-4	1 mile test (7 mi total)
47.	4	4		0	Marathon Goal Race
48.	0	0		0	4-6 miles
49.	2	2		0	6-8 miles (social run)
50.	4	4		2	5 miles or fun race
51.	4	4		3	10-12 (scenic or social)
52.	4	4		4	5 miles or 5K fun race

"C Plan" (Tues) (for those who've run several marathons, and want to improve to the maximum Veterans					Key Weekend Run
Week#	CD	Acg	Pace(p)/Speed(s)	Hills	Speed or Long Run or Race
1.	4	4		3	3mi
2.	5	5		4	4mi
3.	6	6		5	5mi
4.	7	7		6	6mi
5.	8	8		7	7mi(with 1 mi test)
6.	8	8		8	8mi
7.	8	8	4x400(10Ks)	8	9mi
8.	8	8	6x400(10Ks)	7	5mi(with 1mi test)
9.	6	6	8x400(10Ks)	5	10mi
10.	6	6	10x400(10Ks)	4	5K race + 3mi easy
11.	4	4	12x400(10Ks)	2	12mi
12.	4	4	14x400(10Ks)	2	5K race plus 2 mi easy
13.	4	4	16x400(10Ks)	0	14 mi
14.	4	4	18x400(10Ks)	2	1 mi test (5mi total)
15.	4	4	20x400(10Ks)	0	16 mi
16.	4	4	22x400(10Ks)	3	3x800 (half-s)
17.	4	4		0	18 mi
18.	4	4	4x400(10Kp)	2	5-6x800 (half-s)
19.	4	4	4x400(10Kp)	2	10K Goal Race
20.	4	4		0	18 mi

21.	4	4	2x400(half-p))	2	7-9x800(half-s)
22.	4	4	3x400(half-p)	0	9-11x800(half-s)
23.	4	4	1 x 800(half-p)	0	19-20 mi
24.	4	4		0	11-13x800(half-s)
25.	4	4	4x400(5K speed)	2	1 mile test (5 mi total)
26.	4	4	6x400(5K speed)	2	Half Marathon Goal
27.	4	4		0	4 mi—EASY WEEK
28.	4	4	8x400(5K speed)	2	15 mi
29.	4	4	10x400(5K speed)	2	1 mi test (5 mi total)
30.	4	4	12X400(5K speed)	2	17 miles
31.	4	4	14x400(5K speed)	2	4x1mile (m-s)
32.	4	4	3 x 1 mi (m-p)	2	5K Goal Race
33.	4	4		0	20 miles
34.	4	4	3x1mile(m-p)	2	6 x 1 mile (m-s)
35.	4	4	3x1mile(m-p)	2	8x1mi (m-s)
36.	4	4		0	23 miles
37.	4	4	3x1mile(m-p)	2	10x1mi (m-s)
38.	4	4	2x1mile(m-p)	2	1 mile test (6 mi total)
39.	4	4		0	26 miles
40.	4	4	2x1mile(m-p)	2	8 mi easy
41.	4	4	2x1mile(m-p)	2	12 x 1 mi (m-s)
42.	4	4	2x1mile(m-p)	2	1 mile test (8 mi total)
43.	4	4		0	29 miles
44.	4	4		2	4 x 1 mi
45.	4	4	2 x 1 mi (m-p)	0	14 x 1 mi (m-s)
46.	4	4	2 x 1 mi (m-p)	2-4	1 mile test (7 mi total)
47.	4	4		0	Marathon Goal Race
48.	0	0		0	4-6 miles
49.	2	2		1	6-8 miles (social run)
50.	4	4		2	10-12 mi (scenic run)
51.	4	4		3	5 mi or run race
52.	4	4		4	12 mi (social or scenic)

Week # 1

	Mon	Tues	Wed	Thurs	Fri	Sat	Sun
A Plan	off	10 min 2C	off	15 min 0 hills	off	off	1 mile
B Plan	off	20-25 min 2CD 2Acg	off/XT	25-30 min 1 hills	XT or 20 min of running	off	2 miles
C Plan	off	30-45 min 4CD 4Acg	off/XT	30 min 4CD 4Acg	45-60 min 3 hills	off	3 miles

1. The running this week should be nice and easy. If you have had a layoff for a week or more before beginning this program, take an easy week or two to get back into regular running, building back the amounts to those in the schedule above.

2. Even the Acg (acceleration-gliders) should be gentle increases in pace—no sprinting. Run the acceleration part of these just slightly faster than a jog.

3. The goal of the cadence drills (CD), is to increase your turnover rate—not your speed. Stay light on your feet, and just count the steps. Your goal is to increase by one or two extra counts on each one. You will get a little faster as a result of the extra steps—as a by-product of the drill.

4. "B" and "C" runners are doing hill training this week. Mark the distance of the hill by walking down from the top: "B" 100-200, "C" 200-300 steps. Keep shortening

your stride as you run up the hill. It's OK to huff and puff a little as you go up the hill.

5. **Fat-burning tip:** Get a good step counter. Count the number of steps that you take each day, including your running days. Record the number of steps in your journal.

6. If you are starting to cross train, I recommend doing 5 minutes of an activity, resting for 15-20 minutes and then doing 5 more minutes. On each cross training session, afterward you could increase by 3 or 4 additional minutes on each segment.

Week # 2

	Mon	Tues	Wed	Thurs	Fri	Sat	Sun
A Plan	off	15 min 3C 2Acg	off	18 min 0 hills	off	off	1.5 mile
B Plan	off	25-30 min 3CD 3Acg	off/XT	25-30 min 2 hills	XT or 20 min of running	off	3 miles
C Plan	off	30-45 min 5CD 5Acg	off/XT	30 min 5CD 5Acg	45-60 min 4 hills	off	4 miles

1. You may be tempted to increase pace when you're feeling good. Resist this temptation. Continue running easily—and enjoy every run.

2. The most important part of the Acg is the gliding or coasting after the acceleration. Relax, let your feet touch lightly, and use the momentum as you slow down gradually. (read more about Acg in the "drills" chapter)

3. Be sure to write down any unusual aches or pains in your journal that could be a preliminary sign of injury.

4. "B"runners will be doing hill training this week. Mark the distance of the hill by walking down from the top: 100-200 steps. Keep shortening your stride as you run up the hill. It's OK to huff and puff a little as you run up the hill. Walk down the hill and take as much rest as you want between hills.

5. Cross training modes that are best for running are 1) water running, and 2) cross country ski machines (like nordic track).

6. **Fat-burning tip:** Once you have established how many steps per day you are averaging (see last week's fat-burning tip), try to increase by 500 more steps per day, on the average, for this week.

Week # 3

	Mon	Tues	Wed	Thurs	Fri	Sat	Sun
A Plan	off	20 min 4C 3Acg	off	20 min 0 hills	off	off	2 miles
B Plan	off	25-30 min 4CD 4Acg	off/XT	25-30 min 3 hills	XT or 20 min of running	off	4 miles
C Plan	off	30-45 min 6CD 6Acg	off/XT	30-35 min 6CD 6Acg	45-60 min 5 hills	off	5 miles

1. Your primary goal is to feel good at the end of each run. When in doubt, slow down at the beginning and insert more walk breaks. This is the "base building phase" during which your muscles, tendons and other physiological elements adapt to running. Make the adaptation gentle!

2. When you accelerate on the Acg, don't stretch out your stride very much. Pick up the turnover of the feet, and avoid tension in the legs, back, neck, etc. In other words, keep the leg muscles relaxed.

3. As you note the daily run in the journal, record your thoughts and feelings—you'll enjoy reading these later.

4. On long runs, you want to finish with the sensation that you could have gone for another mile or two.

5. **Fat-burning tip:** Continue to watch your step count each day, and find times when you normally would be sitting or standing, to walk around and add steps.

6. Be sure to write down what you did in your training journal.

7. Those who have been doing cross training, continue what has worked for you. Cross Training (XT) is optional, using exercises that don't fatigue the calf muscles. Avoid any exercise that adversely affects your run the next day.

8. The day before long runs is a good day to rest from exercise.

Week # 4

	Mon	Tues	Wed	Thurs	Fri	Sat	Sun
A Plan	off	20-25 min 4C 4Acg	off	20-25 min 1 hill	off	off	2.5 miles
B Plan	off	25-30 min 5CD 5Acg	off/XT	25-30 min 4 hills	XT or 20 min of running	off	5 miles
C Plan	off	30-45 min 7CD 7Acg	off/XT	30-35 min 7CD 7Acg	45-60 min 6 hills	off	6 miles

1. Remember that regularity is important. If it is a running day, and you don't have much time, just get out and run-walk for 5-10 minutes. This will maintain most of your running adaptations.

2. The acceleration on the Acg should be gentle and relaxed—don't push the pace, and never sprint. Let the pace increase naturally as your legs turnover quicker.

3. Don't try to start each CD at the count that you left off on your last session. It is OK to record the number of counts from each session, but start with a clean slate on each session.

4. "A" runners begin hill training this week. Walk down from the top of the hill: 50-100 walking steps and mark the start of your hill. Just run up a little bit faster than a jog, increase pace near the top by quicker turnover of the feet, and go slightly over the top of the hill. Walk down the hill. Use a short stride as you go up the hill.

5. **Fat-burning tip:** Look at some of the websites that help you manage food intake, such as www.fitday.com As you use this, you will have the potential to gain control over the income side of the food equation.

Week # 5

	Mon	Tues	Wed	Thurs	Fri	Sat	Sun
A Plan	off	20-25 min 4C 4Acg	off	20-25 min 2 hills	off	off	3 miles
B Plan	off	30 min 6CD 6Acg	off/XT	30 min 5 hills	XT or 20 min of running	off	6 miles with 1 mile test
C Plan	off	30-45 min 8CD 8Acg	off/XT	30-35 min 8CD 8Acg	45-60 min 7 hills	off	7 miles with 1 mile test

1. Hills: Keep your feet low to the ground, and shorten stride as you go up the hill. Pick up the turnover of your feet to work a bit harder. It's OK to be huffing a puffing a bit at the top—but no sprinting. Run slightly over the top. Walk down the hill.

2. Walk for 5 min before you start running—then jog and walk more often than usual for about 10 minutes as a warm up.

3. On the long run, take more walk breaks as necessary to make it more enjoyable.

4. This is the week for the first one mile test for "B" and "C" runners. Get a good warm-up, including CD and Acg. On a track, this is a 4 lap run, and you can insert short walk breaks on each lap if you wish. Most runners run a faster mile by doing this. You should be huffing and puffing on the last lap. Finish the test feeling like you could only run about half a lap more at the current pace. Reverse the warm-up, for a warm down. In your journal, record your time at the end of each lap, and your walk break—so that you can adjust in future tests, if needed.

5. Cross training: Remember that to maintain your cross training exercise adaptations, you need to do each of these exercises, at least once a week for 10 min each. If you skip weeks, then reduce the amount you are doing on each cross training segment.

6. Fat-burning tip: Try to keep increasing your daily average of steps by 500, each week. Some days will be lower than others—that's OK. On the days when you can get in more walking, go for it.

Week # 6

	Mon	Tues	Wed	Thurs	Fri	Sat	Sun
A Plan	off	20 min 4C 4Acg	off	20 min 2 hills	off	off	3.5 miles
B Plan	off	25 min 7CD 7Acg	off/XT H$_2$O run	25 min 6 hills	XT	off	7 miles
C Plan	off	30 min 8CD 8Acg	off/XT H$_2$Orun	30 min 8CD 8Acg	45 min 8 hills	off	8 miles

1. This week will be a slightly easier week, to let your leg muscles "catch up".

2. Be sure to take the day off of any strenuous running, the day before long runs.

3. Hills: Start each hill at a jog, and gradually increase the turnover of your feet and legs, using a stride that becomes shorter as you go up the hill.

4. Each run is like a piece in a giant pyramid puzzle. You are in the "building base" part of your training pyramid. Even when running slowly or running only a few repetitions you are making the adaptations that you'll need later: you're improving the internal engineering of the muscles and tendons.

5. **Fat-burning tip:** Some cross training exercises will help you burn fat more effectively than others. Choose ones that will elevate your temperature (so that you sweat), use a large number of muscle cells, and can be gradually increased to 45 minutes or more.

6. Water running (H$_2$Orun) is the only cross training activity that I know improve your running. Do this in the deep end of the pool, using a flotation belt. Start with a 5 minute segment, rest for 10-20 minutes, and do another 5 minute segment. In order to increase the benefit from this exercise, add 3 additional minutes to each segment during next week's workout, and do your water running once or twice a week.

Week # 7

	Mon	Tues	Wed	Thurs	Fri	Sat	Sun
A Plan	off	25 min 4C 4Acg	off	25 min 2 hills	off	off	3 miles (with 1 mile test)
B Plan	off	25-30 min 8CD 8Acg	off/XT H₂Orun	25-30 min 7 hills	XT or 20 min of running	off	8 miles
C Plan	off	30-45 min 8CD 8Acg 4x400 (10K speed)	off/XT H₂Orun	30-35 min 8CD	45-60 min 8 hills 8Acg	off	9 miles

1. "C" runners will begin 10K speedwork. After an easy 10 + min warm-up, then CD, then Acg, run a 400 (one lap around a track) and walk for 200 meters. Repeat for a total of 4 x 400. Run each 400 at a pace that is 5-7 seconds faster than your goal pace in the 10K (10K time divided by 25, then subtract 5-7 seconds).

2. Speedwork is provided for those who want to improve their times in the 10K. If you have no desire to improve 10K speed, just run easily for the time noted on the schedule on that Tuesday.

3. This is the week for the first one mile test for "A" runners. Get a good warm-up, including CD and Acg. On a track, this is a 4 lap run, and you can insert short walk breaks on each lap if you wish. Most runners run a faster mile by doing this. You should be huffing and puffing on the last lap. Finish the test feeling like you could only run about half a lap at the current pace. Reverse the warm-up, for a warm down.

4. It's possible, even on the toughest of running days, to find some enjoyment in every run. You may to use your imagination to do this, but having some moments of fun will magnify your enjoyment of running over the years. At the least, you'll have more endorphins to make you feel good after the run.

	Mon	Tues	Wed	Thurs	Fri	Sat	Sun
A Plan	off	25 min 4C 4Acg	off H₂Orun	25 min 3 hills	off	off	4 miles
B Plan	off	30-35 min 8CD 8Acg 4x400 (10K speed)	off/XT H₂Orun	30-35 min 6 hills	XT or 20 min of running	off	4 miles (with 1 mile test)
C Plan	off	30-45 min 8CD 8Acg 6x400 (10K speed)	off/XT H₂Orun	30-35 min 8CD 8Acg	45-60 min 7 hills	off	5 miles (with 1 mile test)

1. "B" runners will begin 10K speedwork. After an easy 10 + min warm-up, then CD, then Acg, run a 400 (one lap around a track) and walk for 200 meters. Repeat for a total of 4 x 400. Run each 400 at a pace that is 5-7 seconds faster than your goal pace in the 10K.

2. Don't ever try to run through pain. Even running one more lap, or one more easy mile, at the beginning stages of an injury, can produce enough damage to put you out of commission for weeks or months. It is always safer to stop and treat the painful area. When in doubt, talk to your doctor.

3. "B" and "C" runners will run another one mile test. Look over the pacing of your last one mile test and improve it. Make any strategic changes that you believe could produce a faster time than your last test. The only exception is not to sprint at the end. The one mile test is an excellent predictor of your per mile performance on longer events (add 33 seconds for 5K pace, multiply by

the following for the other per mile paces: 1.15 for the 10K * 1.2 for the half marathon * 1.3 for the marathon.

4. Here's how "B" and "C" runners can compute their pace for the 400 repeats:

One mile test time x 1.15 divided by 4. That is the per mile pace of your goal 10K. Subtract 10-20 seconds (leap of faith goal workout pace).

5. Don't ever sprint at the end of any run. Sprinting is running all out, which often results in injury or a much longer recovery afterwards. The preferred way of speeding up your time is to increase pace during the middle of the race or test.

6. Fat-burning warm-up/warm-down: Walk an extra 5-10 minutes before and after you start/finish running (more than your usual warm up). This not only burns more fat, it helps the legs get prepared better before, and lets them down gently afterwards.

Week # 9

	Mon	Tues	Wed	Thurs	Fri	Sat	Sun
A Plan	off	25 min 4C 4Acg	off	25 min 3 hills	off	off	4.5 miles
B Plan	off	30-40 min 6CD 6Acg 6x400 (10K speed)	off/XT H$_2$Orun	30 min 4 hills	XT or 20 min of easy running	off	9 miles
C Plan	off	30-45 min 6CD 6Acg 8x400 (10K speed)	off/XT H$_2$Orun	30-35 min 6CD 6Acg	45-60 min 5 hills	off	10 miles

1. Make sure that you are taking enough rest between your hill repeats or the 400s. Walking for 200 meters is the recommendation after a 400. After each hill, walk down.

2. It is not a good idea, at the end of the workout, to lengthen your stride. This often produces shin pain, sore quads, and other pain in your "weak links." Try to maintain or increase turnover, while shortening the stride length. You will be practicing this on your Acg.

3. If you seem to be a bit more tired, when doing the same workout each week, reduce the amount of running you're doing on Thursday.

4. This week, focus on the warmdown at the end of each run. During that 10 minute period you can enjoy the "glow" from the run. This can be one of the best times of the day.

Week # 10

	Mon	Tues	Wed	Thurs	Fri	Sat	Sun
A Plan	off	30 min 4C 4Acg	off	30 min 3 hills	off	off	3 miles (including 1 mile test)
B Plan	off	30-40 min 6CD 6Acg 8x400 (10K speed)	off/XT H_2Orun	30 min 4 hills	XT or 20 min of easy running	off	5K test race plus 2 miles easy
C Plan	off 6CD	30-45 min H_2Orun 6Acg 10x400 (10K speed)	off/XT 6CD	30-35 min	45-60 min 4 hills 6Acg	off	5K race plus 3 miles easy

1. "A" runners should look over their last one mile test and then try to run faster on this one. Look at the pacing, and the walk breaks and adjust them for a better performance. Don't sprint! The time in the one mile test can predict your pace per mile in longer events: 5K—add 33 seconds * 10K—multiply by 1.15 * half marathon—multiply by 1.2 * marathon—multiply by 1.3

2. On the last part of the Acg, the "glide", you will learn how to relax—even though you are running faster than your normal running pace. Gliding conserves resources, while you maintain a fast pace.

3. The test races (one mile, 5K) give you a taste of what it will be like in your goal race. They allow you to adjust pacing and try various ways of using the walk breaks, and the Acg's.

4. This is the first 5K race for "B" and "C" runners—be sure to read the section on "Race Day" in this book. Run the first mile a bit slower than you think you can average, and pick up the pace of each successive mile. Most of those who run 7 min/mi or slower will benefit from a walk break at each mile, as follows:

7 min pace—10-15 seconds each mile

7:30 pace—15-20 seconds each mile

8:00 pace—20-25 seconds each mile

8:30 pace—25-30 seconds each mile

9:00 pace—25-30 seconds each mile

9:30 pace—30-35 seconds each mile

10:00 pace—30-35 seconds each mile

10:30 pace—30-40 seconds each mile

11:00 pace—35-40 seconds each mile

11:30 pace—40-45 seconds each mile

12:00 pace—45-50 seconds each mile

12:30 pace—50-55 seconds each mile

13:00 pace—55-60 seconds each mile

Week # 11

	Mon	Tues	Wed	Thurs	Fri	Sat	Sun
A Plan	off	30 min 4C 4Acg	off H₂Orun	30 min 3 hills	off	off	5 miles
B Plan	off	30-40 min 4CD 4cg 10x400 (10K speed)	off/XT H₂Orun	30 min 4 hills	XT or 20 min of easy running	off	10 miles
C Plan	off	30-45 min 4CD 4Acg 12x400 (10K speed)	off/XT H₂Orun	30-35 min 4CD 4Acg	45-60 min 2 hills	off	12 miles

1. "A" runners are beginning to increase distance. Be careful not to run the long runs too fast. Follow the suggestions as noted in the long run pacing guidelines.

2. "B" and "C" runners who are slowing down at the end of the Tuesday speed workouts should run the first 2-3 400s slower than the pace they intend to average. On the last few, try to run one second faster than average.

3. A slowdown in pace on any run means that you were running too fast in the beginning, for that day—unless there was a dramatic increase in temperature at the end of the run.

4. During hot weather, it often helps to have a good electrolyte beverage, like Accelerade, to sip between repetitions during speed workouts. Dilute the mix by adding about 25-50% more water. Drink only 2-4 oz every 2-3 laps.

Week # 12

	Mon	Tues	Wed	Thurs	Fri	Sat	Sun
A Plan	off	30 min 4C 4Acg	off	30 min 4 hills	off	off	5.5 miles
B Plan	off	30-40 min 4CD 4cg 12x400 (10K speed)	off/XT H₂Orun	30 min 2 hills	XT or 20 min of easy running	off	5K race + 2 miles easy
C Plan	off	30-45 min 4CD 4Acg 14x400 (10K speed)	off/XT H₂Orun	30-35 min 4CD 4Acg	45-60 min 2 hills	off	5K race + 2 miles easy

1. "B" and "C" runners will be running the second 5K race. Look back at your mile pace on the first 5K, and adjust to improve. If your first mile was faster than your last, slow the first one down by a few seconds. Most runners run faster when they slow down enough to run the last mile faster.

2. After 5K races, the extra mileage noted (2 miles this week) can be done immediately, or can be run as a second workout later in the day.

3. Don't push the pace on the hill repeats. Try to maintain relaxed running form as you quickly step your way to the top.

4. **Fat-burning tip:** If you slow down your easy run days even more, and put more walk breaks, you could add another 10-15 minutes to each.

Week # 13

	Mon	Tues	Wed	Thurs	Fri	Sat	Sun
A Plan	off	30 min 4C 4Acg	off	30 min 2-3 hills	off	off	5K race
B Plan	off	30-40 min 4CD 4cg 14x400 (10K speed)	off/XT H$_2$Orun	30 min 1 hill	XT or 20 min of easy running	off	12 miles
C Plan	off	30-45 min 4CD 4Acg 16x400 (10K speed)	off/XT H$_2$Orun	30-35 min 4CD 4Acg	45-60 min 1 hill	off	14 miles

1. This is the first 5K race for "A" runners. Be sure to read the "Race Day" section of this book. Run the first mile a bit slower than you think you can average, and pick up the pace of each successive mile. Most of you will benefit from a 30-60 second walk break after each mile. Here are my recommendations for walk breaks during the 5K, based upon pace:

7 min pace—10-15 seconds each mile

7:30 pace—15-20 seconds each mile

8:00 pace—20-25 seconds each mile

8:30 pace—25-30 seconds each mile

9:00 pace—25-30 seconds each mile

9:30 pace—30-35 seconds each mile

10:00 pace—30-35 seconds each mile

10:30 pace—30-40 seconds each mile

11:00 pace—35-40 seconds each mile

11:30 pace—40-45 seconds each mile

12:00 pace—45-50 seconds each mile

12:30 pace—50-55 seconds each mile

13:00 pace—55-60 seconds each mile

2. Remember to slow down the long run, even more, when the temperature rises above 60°F. For every 5 degree temperature increase, slow down by 30 seconds a mile.

3. Be aware of any ache or pain in an area where you have had injuries or lingering soreness before. If there is inflammation, loss of function, or pain that doesn't go away—stop the workout. Trying to run through an injury greatly increases the damage.

4. It doesn't take much time to make quick notes in your journal about unusual things that can help you later: an unexpected experience, a crazy thought from your right brain. Be particularly sensitive to any ache in a body part where you tend to get injured or sore. Write this down so that you can see patterns that may be causing the problem.

Week # 14

	Mon	Tues	Wed	Thurs	Fri	Sat	Sun
A Plan	off	30 min 4C 4Acg	off	30 min 2 hills	off	off	6 miles
B Plan	off	30-45 min 4CD 4cg 16x400 (10K speed)	off/XT H$_2$Orun	30 min 0 hills	XT or 20 min of easy running	off	1 mile test (5 miles total)
C Plan	off	30-45 min 4CD 4Acg 18x400 (10K speed)	off/XT H$_2$Orun	30-35 min 4CD 4Acg	45-60 min	off	1 mile test (5 miles total) 2 hills

1. Those in the "B" & "C" plans are nearing the end of the 10K speed schedule. Remember that the most important part of the program is to complete the number of repetitions, in the time assigned. If you need to walk more between each 400 repetition, do so.

2. If you are slowing down during the last lap of the one mile test, try running the first lap at the pace that you ran the last lap, in your last test. Another tactical move is to walk a bit more after each lap.

3. **Fat-burning tip:** Park your car a few blocks farther away from everywhere you go: work, supermarket, running trail, etc. The extra walking steps, on every trip, add up quickly.

Week # 15

	Mon	Tues	Wed	Thurs	Fri	Sat	Sun
A Plan	off	30 min 4C 4Acg	off	30 min 4 hills	off	off	2 miles
B Plan	off	30-45 min 4CD 4cg 18x400 (10K speed)	off/XT H_2Orun	30 min 0 hills	XT	off	14 miles
C Plan	off	30-45 min 4CD 4Acg 20x400 (10K speed)	off/XT H_2Orun	30 min 4CD 4Acg	30 min 0 hills	off	16 miles

1. Keep the long runs slow! This is particularly important for those in the "B" and "C" plans who are running a peak 400 meter workout and a long run. Remember that the long runs should be run at least 2 min per mile slower than your current one mile test is predicting for marathon pace (mile test time x 1.3 plus 2 minutes).

2. Even if you're feeling strong at the end of a speed workout or long run, don't increase the pace. There are many injuries that result from doing this.

3. Avoid the temptation to lift your knees at the end of a hard run—this will produce sore quadraceps muscles. Keep feet low to the ground and pick up the cadence. You're learning how to do this on your CD drills.

4. "A" runners have an easy week this week. Relax, and let your body rebuild stronger!

	Mon	Tues	Wed	Thurs	Fri	Sat	Sun
A Plan	off	30 min 4C 4Acg	off	30 min 0 hills	off	off	7 miles
B Plan	off	30-45 min 4CD 4cg 20x400 (10K speed)	off/XT H₂Orun	30 min 0 hills	XT	off	3x800 (half-s)
C Plan	off	30-45 min 4CD 4Acg 22x400 (10K speed)	off/XT H₂Orun	30-35 min 4CD 4Acg	30 min 0 hills	off	3x800 (half-s)

1. "B" & "C" runners will be starting speed training for the half marathon. Because you are also finishing up your 10K speed training, it is OK to take a 4-5 min walk between the 800s (instead of the usual 3 min walk).

2. Don't ever try to run through pain. When you experience pain in a muscle, joint, tendon, etc., which does not go away with liberal walking, stop the workout. Treat the pain as if it were an injury.

3. If during some of your runs you feel like you are stuck in a rut, schedule a social run with a friend, or run in a scenic area that you really enjoy.

Week # 17

	Mon	Tues	Wed	Thurs	Fri	Sat	Sun
A Plan	off	30 min 4C 4Acg	off	30 min 3-4 hills	off	off	1 mile test (3mi total)
B Plan	off	30 min 4CD 4cg	off/XT H_2Orun	30 min 2-3 hills	XT	off	16 miles
C Plan	off	30-35 min 4CD 4Acg	off/XT H_2Orun	30 min 4CD 4Acg	30 min 2-3 hills	off	18 miles

1. "B" and "C" runners can take a break from speedwork this week. Remember that you cannot run too slow on the long run. On the long run this week, run 3 min/mi slower than predicted marathon pace (mile test x 1.3) with more liberal walk breaks. This should allow the week to be an easy week for your legs.

2. "A" runners should continue to adjust pacing on each lap of the mile test. Recommended strategy is to have the slowest lap (by 1-2 seconds) be the first lap. The fastest lap should be the last lap.

3. This would be a good week to look back at the last 4 weeks of training in your training journal. Look at the items that you would like to change, and make the changes starting this week!

Week # 18

	Mon	Tues	Wed	Thurs	Fri	Sat	Sun
A Plan	off	30 min 4C 4Acg	off	30 min 0 hills	off	off	8 miles
B Plan	off	30 min 4CD 4cg 4x400 (10K pace)	off/XT H₂Orun	30 min 2 hills	XT or 20 min of easy running	off	5-6x800 (half-s)
C Plan	off	30-45 min 4CD 4Acg 4x400 (10K pace)	off/XT H₂Orun	30-35 min 4CD 4Acg	45-60 min 2 hills	off	5-6x800 (half-s)

1. "A" runners should run very slowly (and take more frequent walk breaks) on the long run this week. This will allow the body to experience an "easy week" even while the long run is increasing. We want your legs to be strong for your 10K race next week.

2. "B" and "C" runners will be increasing the number of 800s toward your half marathon goal. Make sure that you don't run the first few of these 800s too fast. The pace should be 15 seconds faster than your goal pace for a half mile, in your half marathon goal race.

3. "B" and "C" runners will be running 400s on Tuesdays at 10K pace. Try to get into a "groove" of running easily at this pace.

	Mon	Tues	Wed	Thurs	Fri	Sat	Sun
A Plan	off	30 min 4C 4Acg	off	30 min 0 hills	off	off	10K race
B Plan	off	30 min 4CD 4cg 4x400 (10K pace)	off/XT H₂Orun	30 min 2 hills	XT or 20 min of easy running	off	10K race
C Plan	off	30-45 min 4CD 4Acg 4x400 (10K pace)	off/XT H₂Orun	30-35 min 4CD 4Acg	45-60 min 2 hills	off	10K race

1. This is 10K race weekend for all levels. Top priority is to enjoy the experience, while running strong to the finish. Read the "Race Day" section of this book. Other goals are the following:
   - finish in the upright position
   - with a smile on your face
   - wanting to do another race

2. To predict your pace, take your average time in your one mile tests and multiply by 1.15. This is a good prediction for your average per mile pace for the 10K, if the temperature is 65°F or below. It helps to run 10-20 seconds slower than this pace on the first mile or two. If the temperature is warmer than 65°F, you will not run as fast as you would in cooler temperatures. The best strategy is to be conservative from the beginning.

3. If you have any concerns about your conditioning, slow your pace from the beginning of the 10K race by another 20-30 seconds per mile, for the first 1-2 miles. If you are feeling good between 4 and 5 miles, pick up the pace.

4. If you reach any mile mark faster than the pace you should be running, walk longer to let your time catch up. This should help you avoid a slowdown at the end.

5. Walk breaks can be taken at least every mile. Here is a pace guideline for walk breaks:

8 min—20 sec per mile

9 min—30 sec per mile

10 min—30 sec after 4-5 min of running

11 min—30 sec after 3-4 min of running

12 min—30 sec after 2-3 min of running

13 min—30 sec after 2 min of running

14 min—30 sec after 1-2 min of running

15 min—30 sec after 30-60 seconds of running

16 min—30 sec after 30 seconds of running

Week # 20

	Mon	Tues	Wed	Thurs	Fri	Sat	Sun
A Plan	off	30 min 4C 4Acg	off	30 min 3 hills	off	off	3 miles
B Plan	off	30 min 4CD 4cg	off/XT H₂Orun	30 min 0 hills	XT or 20 min of easy running	off	18 miles
C Plan	off	30-45 min 4CD 4Acg	off/XT H₂Orun	30-35 min 4CD 4Acg	45-60 min 0 hills	off	18 miles

1. "A" runners should take it very easy this week. The hills are the only challenge, so walk down the hill for complete recovery.

2. "B" & "C" runners should pace the 18 miler very slowly. Normally this would mean 2 min/mi slower than predicted by your one mile test average. It is better to slow down another minute or so, particularly if you raced hard last week in the 10K.

3. **Fat-burning tip:** On recovery weeks, and long run weeks you want to reduce the running mileage for quick muscle recovery. You can maintain or increase fat burning by increasing the number of steps you're walking each day. Give that step counter a real workout!

4. Start fine-tuning your breakfast before long runs. Eliminate any foods that could cause you problems. You can avoid a breakfast entirely if you start taking your blood sugar boosting foods (gu or gel products) within the first few miles of your run.

Week # 21

	Mon	Tues	Wed	Thurs	Fri	Sat	Sun
A Plan	off	30 min 4C 4Acg	off	30 min 0 hills	off	off	7.5 miles
B Plan	off	30 min 4CD 4cg 2x800 (half marathon pace)	off/XT H₂Orun	30 min 2 hills	XT or 20 min of easy running	off	7-9x800 (half-s)
C Plan	off	30-45 min 4CD 4Acg 4x800 (half marathon pace)	off/XT H₂Orun	30-35 min 4CD 4Acg	45-60 min 2 hills	off	7-9x800 (half-s)

1. "B" & "C" runners will be running 800s again on the weekend. If you were slowing down at the end of your last 800 workout, run the first few 800 reps slower by 5-10 seconds each—than you did before. Walk for 3 minutes between each

2. "B" & "C" runners will also run some 800s at their projected half marathon pace during the Tuesday workout. Do your usual warm up and warm down. Walk for 3-4 minutes between each. Also practice taking a walk break of 15-30 seconds after running one lap.

3. Remember that the primary goal is to stay injury free. Always eliminate the speed workouts if you think that you might be getting an injury.

4. This is a good time to look ahead in your journal at the next 4 weeks' workouts. This helps you schedule the long workout days around the activities in the rest of your life.

Week # 22

	Mon	Tues	Wed	Thurs	Fri	Sat	Sun
A Plan	off	30 min 4C 4Acg	off	30 min 3-4 hills	off	off	3 miles
B Plan	off	30 min 4CD 4cg 3x800 (half marathon pace)	off/XT H₂Orun	30 min 0 hills	XT or 20 min of easy running	off	9-11x800 (half-speed)
C Plan	off	30-45 min 4CD 4Acg 4x800 (half marathon pace)	off/XT H₂Orun	30-35 min 4CD 4Acg	45-60 min 2 hills	off	9-11x800 (half-speed)

1. "A" runners: you can't run too easy this week, except for the hills. Take it easy otherwise. This is a recovery week.

2. "B" & "C" runners should work on a smooth stride as they get tired. Avoid the temptation of increasing stride length or lifting knees. A fast shuffle is a better tactic.

3. If you miss a week of speed sessions, it is usually fine to jump right back with the program. In this case you should slow down the first two speed repeats to your goal race pace. Then pick up the pace as usually scheduled.

4. You have really made progress! Congratulate yourself!

Week # 23

	Mon	Tues	Wed	Thurs	Fri	Sat	Sun
A Plan	off	30 min 4C 4Acg	off	30 min 0 hills	off	off	9 miles
B Plan	off	30 min 4CD 4cg 2x800 (h.m.p.)	off/XT H$_2$Orun	30 min 0 hills	XT or 20 min of easy running	off	19-20 miles
C Plan	off	30-45 min 4CD 4Acg 2x800 (h.m.p.)	off/XT H$_2$Orun	30-35 min 4CD 4Acg	30 min 0 hills	off	19-20 miles

1. Remember to adjust pace when the temperature rises above 60°F: slow down by an additional 30 sec a mile for every 5 degree increase above 60°F. Take more frequent walk breaks also.

2. The long runs are building for "B" and "C" runners. You cannot go too slow on these runs. The slower you run, the faster you recover.

3. **Fat-burning tip:** Try to eat 8-10 times a day. You will not only burn more fat off your body this way (assuming the same calorie consumption in 2-3 meals a day). Eating more frequently gives you more energy and motivation for adding walking steps, taking the stairs, parking farther away from work, stores, etc.

4. If you have problems getting out of bed for the early morning runs, or getting out the door after work on a running day, read the mental toughness section of this book. By breaking down the challenge into a series of small steps you can make the movement from one step to the other an almost automatic experience.

Week # 24

	Mon	Tues	Wed	Thurs	Fri	Sat	Sun
A Plan	off	30 min 4C 4Acg	off	30 min 3-4 hills	off	off	3 miles
B Plan	off	30 min 4CD 4cg	off/XT H₂Orun	30 min 0 hills	XT	off	11-13x800 (half speed)
C Plan	off	30-45 min 4CD 4Acg	off/XT H₂Orun	30-35 min 4CD 4Acg	30 min 0 hills	off	11-13 x 800 (half speed)

1. "A" runners should enjoy this easy week—this is another recovery week.

2. "B" & "C" runners: this is your last workout before the half marathon race. Remember that you don't want to be totally exhausted at the end of your speed repetitions. Stay smooth during the last 3 800s and finish feeling like you could have run another 1 or 2 of them. If you are becoming exhausted, stop the workout. If you had trouble recovering from your last 800 meter workout, walk for 4-5 minutes between each 800.

3. Never run if you have a lung infection. Always check with your doctor when you have an infection, and get clearance to run.

4. There are very few things in life that can make you feel as good as finishing your run. Relax and enjoy your endorphins!

Week # 25

	Mon	Tues	Wed	Thurs	Fri	Sat	Sun
A Plan	off	30 min 4C 4Acg	off	30 min 0 hills	off	off	10.5 miles
B Plan	off	30 min 4CD 4cg 3x400 (5K speed)	off/XT H$_2$Orun	30 min 2 hills	XT or 20 min of easy running	off	1mile test (5 mi total)
C Plan	off	30-45 min 4CD 4Acg 4x400 (5K speed)	off/XT H$_2$Orun	30-35 min 4CD 4Acg	30 min 2 hills	off	1 mile test (5 mi total)

1. "A" runners: you're making great progress in building your long run. Enjoy the 10.5 miler.

2. "B" & "C" runners: You're starting the speed training for a 5K goal race. After each 400, walk for half a lap. Run each 400 faster than goal pace (by 5-7 seconds).

3. "B" & "C" runners should also take it easy this week between the Tuesday workout and the one mile test. You cannot run too slowly on these days.

4. One mile test info: "B" & "C" runners can now tell what their pace should be for their half marathon:

    • take your last 3 one mile test times and compute the average
    • multiply by 1.2—this is a per mile prediction for a hard effort in the half marathon
    • example: one mile test average is 10:00. The predicted half marathon pace is 12 min/mi

- look at the run-walk-run tm section of the book to see what your ratio should be
- it's always better to run slower than this pace for the first 3-6 miles
- adjust for temperature: add 30 seconds a mile for every 5 degrees above 60°F.

5. You are the captain of your running ship. Take charge of your fatigue in advance by slowing down and walking more.

Week # 26

	Mon	Tues	Wed	Thurs	Fri	Sat	Sun
A Plan	off	30 min 4CD 4Acg	off	30 min 2 hills	off	off	1 mile test (3 mi total)
B Plan	off	30 min 4CD 4cg 5x400 (5K speed)	off/XT H$_2$Orun	30 min 2 hills	XT	off	Half Marathon Race
C Plan	off	30-45 min 4CD 4Acg 6x400 (5K speed)	off/XT H$_2$Orun	30-35 min 4CD 4Acg	30 min 2 hills	off	Half Marathon Race

1. "A" runners should see some improvement in their 1 mile test time. Be sure to look back at your pace for the last 2 tests, and make pacing changes as needed. If you're speeding up too much at the end, then run your first two laps a little faster

2. "B" & "C" runners will be running a half marathon race. Remember that it is hard to slow down enough in the beginning. If you find yourself ahead of pace, then walk more during the next mile.

3. **Fat-burning tip:** Even on a day off from running, it's OK to walk. If it is the day before a race or long run, you shouldn't try for 10,000 steps, but a total that is less than you have been averaging.

4. Be sure to add 30 sec/mi for every 5 degrees of temperature increase above 60°F.

Congratulations for a successful half year of running your "plan"!

	Mon	Tues	Wed	Thurs	Fri	Sat	Sun
A Plan	off	30 min 4CD 4Acg	off	30 min	off	off	12 miles
B Plan	off	30 min 4CD 4Acg	off/XT H₂Orun	30 min 0 hills	XT or 20 min of easy running	off	4 miles easy EASY WEEK!
C Plan	off	30-45 min 4CD 4Acg	off/XT H₂Orun	30-35 min 4CD 4Acg	30 min 0 hills	off	4 miles easy

1. "B" & "C" runners should rest and recover this week. Just jog slowly and short, on each running day. You've earned this rest.

2. "A" runners are building distance toward the half marathon. Run the 12 miles very easy.

3. If you are having trouble getting your runs started, do more walking for the first 3 miles.

4. Avoid the temptation to run fast on a slow recovery day...or easy week. You need the rest periods so that you can rebuild stronger.

5. If you have been bothered by a lot of left brain messages, rehearse them in advance. You can also rehearse your automatic response to these messages: "Shut up, left brain, I know you're bluffing" or something like that.

Week # 28

	Mon	Tues	Wed	Thurs	Fri	Sat	Sun
A Plan	off	30 min 4CD 4Acg	off	30 min 3-4 hills	off	off	1 mile test (3mi total)
B Plan	off	30 min 4CD 4cg 7x400 (5K speed)	off/XT H$_2$Orun	30 min 2 hills	XT or 20 min of easy running	off	15 miles
C Plan	off	30-45 min 4CD 4Acg 8x400 (5K speed)	off/XT H$_2$Orun	30-35 min 4CD 4Acg	45-60 min 2 hills	off	15 miles

1. Those in the "B" & "C" plans are at the mid point of the 5K speed schedule. Remember that the most important part of the program is to complete the number of repetitions, in the time assigned. If you need to walk more between each 400 repetition, do so.

2. If you are slowing down during the last lap of the one mile test, try running the first lap at the pace that you ran the last lap, in your last test. Another tactical move is to walk a bit more after each lap.

3. **Reloading Tip:** The best time to reload is within 30 minutes of the finish of a run. My recommendation is a snack (200-300 calories) that is 80% simple carbohydrate and 20% protein. Endurox R4 is has this already formulated for you.

4. It is not a good idea to drink alcohol the night before a long run or hard run of any type.

5. Most runners run faster when they run a negative split. This means that they slowed down enough in the first half so that they could speed up in the second half. During the last third of all of your goal races, you can cut down on the walk breaks or run continuously if you wish. Most runners continue to take walk breaks in some form.

Week # 29

	Mon	Tues	Wed	Thurs	Fri	Sat	Sun
A Plan	off	30 min 4CD 4Acg	off	30 min 0 hills	off	off	13.5 miles
B Plan	off	30 min 4CD 4cg 9x400 (5K speed)	off/XT H₂Orun	30 min 2 hills	XT or 20 min of easy running	off	1 mile test (5 mi total)
C Plan	off	30-45 min 4CD 4Acg 10x400 (5K speed)	off/XT H₂Orun	30-35 min 4CD 4Acg	45-60 min 2 hills	off	1 mile test (5 mi total)

1. It is fine to start your CD and Acg drills at a slower pace. This warms up the tendons, ligaments, muscles, and helps you get into a "groove." By doing these each week, you will improve form and running efficiency.

2. "A" runners should ensure that they run slowly enough on their long run this week. You are getting into good shape and many runners go too fast at this point—and struggle at the end. Watch your pace.

3. "B" and "C" runners should run very slowly between the Tuesday workout and the one mile test.

4. Schedule a social run with friends, every week if possible. These allow you to catch up on the gossip.

	Mon	Tues	Wed	Thurs	Fri	Sat	Sun
A Plan	off	30 min 4CD 4Acg	off	30 min 3-4 hills	off	off	3 miles
B Plan	off	30 min 4CD 4cg 11x400 (5K speed)	off/XT H$_2$Orun	30 min 2 hills	XT or 20 min of easy running	off	17 miles
C Plan	off	30-45 min 4CD 4Acg 12x400 (5K speed)	off/XT H$_2$Orun	30-35 min 4CD 4Acg	45-60 min 2 hills	off	17 miles

1. "B" & "C" runners are running a significant number of 400's while also running long on the weekends. It's always best to slow down the long runs, and walk more, in this situation. Instead of slowing down 2 min/mi slower than marathon goal pace, use a 3 min/mi slowdown.

2. Be aware of any ache or pain in an area where you have had injuries or lingering soreness before. If there is inflammation, loss of function, or pain that doesn't go away—stop the workout. Trying to run through an injury greatly increases the damage.

3. If you haven't started your motivational training, read the mental toughness section of this book. Having a strategy can help you through the most difficult of times.

4. Ratios of run-walk-run tm for almost any distance:

16-18 min/mi—1-1

14-15 min/mi—either 1-1 or 2-1

12-13 min/mi—2-1

10-11 min/mi—3-1

9:30 min/mi—4-1

9 min/mi—5-1 to 7-1 (or 30 second walk/3-4 min run)

8:30 min/mi—30 sec walk/4 min run

8 min/mi—30 sec walk/5 min run

Week # 31

	Mon	Tues	Wed	Thurs	Fri	Sat	Sun
A Plan	off	30 min 4CD 4Acg	off	30 min 0 hills	off	off	15 miles
B Plan	off	30 min 4CD 4cg 13x400 (5K speed)	off/XT H$_2$Orun	30 min 2 hills	XT or 20 min of easy running	off	4 x 1 mi (marathon speed)
C Plan	off	30-45 min 4CD 4Acg 14x400 (5K speed)	off/XT H$_2$Orun	30-35 min 4CD 4Acg	45-60 min 2 hills	off	4 x 1 mi (marathon speed)

1. "B" and "C" runners will be starting marathon speedwork: one mile repeats. Run each of these 30 seconds per mile faster than your goal pace in the marathon. Walk for 5 min between each. Be sure to do the usual 10-15 min of warm up and warm down—as before any speed workout. It's best to use the same walk-run ratio you plan to use in the marathon.

2. "B" and "C" runners are doing faster, 5K speed on Tuesday, and slower speed on Saturday. If you need to take more rest between each repetition—take it.

3. Be sure to drink 3-6 oz of water or a sports drink like Accelerade between the mile repeats, or after 2-3 of the 400s.

4. Avoid lengthening your stride at the end of your speed repetitions. This can produce hamstring, lower back or Ilio-tibial band injuries.

5. Reward yourself with a 200-300 calorie snack within 30 min after any workout that feels hard for you—especially these speed sessions. The best recovery food is a drink or smoothie that has 80% of the calories in simple carbohydrate and 20% of the carbs in protein. You can blend in fruit and yogurt if you wish.

	Mon	Tues	Wed	Thurs	Fri	Sat	Sun
A Plan	off	30 min 4 CD 4 Acg	off	30 min 3-4 hills	off	off	1 mile test (3 mi total)
B Plan	off	30 min 4CD 4Acg 3 x 1 mi (marathon pace)	off/XT H$_2$Orun	30 min 2 hills	XT or 20 min of easy running	off	5K Goal Race
C Plan	off	30-45 min 4CD 4Acg (marathon pace)	off/XT H$_2$Orun	30-35 min 4CD 4Acg 3 x 1 mi	45-60 min 2 hills	off	5K Goal Race

1. "B" and "C" runners will be running the 5K goal race this weekend. To predict your per mile pace for this, add 33 seconds to the pace of your average one mile test. It is always better to run a bit more slowly than this during the first mile—by 5-10 seconds.

2. Most runners will run faster times in the 5K when they take a walk break after each mile. Here are the recommended walk breaks:

7 min pace—10-15 seconds each mile	
7:30 pace—15-20 seconds each mile	
8:00 pace—20-25 seconds each mile	
8:30 pace—25-30 seconds each mile	
9:00 pace—25-30 seconds each mile	
9:30 pace—30-35 seconds each mile	
10:00 pace—30-35 seconds each mile	

10:30 pace—30-40 seconds each mile

11:00 pace—35-40 seconds each mile

11:30 pace—40-45 seconds each mile

12:00 pace—45-50 seconds each mile

12:30 pace—50-55 seconds each mile

13:00 pace—55-60 seconds each mile

3. "B" and "C" runners will be starting their marathon pace segments this week, on Tuesdays. These one mile repeats should be run at your goal marathon pace, taking the walk breaks as you plan to take them in the marathon. Walk for 3-5 min between each.

4. On most of the longer speed sessions and longest long runs you will reach a point where you would rather stop right there. A primary strategy that works for many is to say "I can do one more." As you keep saying (and doing) one more, you break through barriers and prepare yourself for success.

Week # 33

	Mon	Tues	Wed	Thurs	Fri	Sat	Sun
A Plan	off	30 min 4CD 4Acg	off	30 min	off	off	Half Marathon Race
B Plan	off	30 min 4CD 4cg	off/XT H₂Orun	30 min 0 hills	XT or 20 min of easy running	off	20 Miles
C Plan	off	30-45 min 4CD 4Acg	off/XT H₂Orun	30-35 min 4CD 4Acg	45-60 min 0 hills	off	20 miles

1. "A" runners will be running a half marathon race this weekend. To predict pace, take your average one mile test times and multiply by 1.2 (a 10 min mile test, means a 12 minute pace in the half marathon). As always, it is fine to run more slowly than this pace—especially in the beginning, by 20-30 seconds a mile.

2. Slow down in the heat! Whether in races or long runs, you must adjust for heat. For every 5 degrees of increased temperature above 60°F, slow the pace by 30 seconds a mile.

3. Watch what you eat the day before and the morning of your long runs. The eating patterns you establish will be the ones you can fine-tune and use during your race itself. It's best to eat a series of small meals or snacks, every 2 hours or so, the day before. Avoid foods that could cause you problems such as fat, protein, high fiber, dairy, and problem foods for you. It is never a good idea to eat a big meal the night before a long run.

4. Read the "dirty tricks" section of the "mental toughness" chapter of this book. You will benefit from this tactic—they're fun.

Week # 34

	Mon	Tues	Wed	Thurs	Fri	Sat	Sun
A Plan	off	30 min 4CD 4Acg	off H₂Orun	30 min 2 hills	off	off	3 miles easy
B Plan	off	30 min 4CD 4Acg 3 x 1 mi (marathon pace)	off/XT H₂Orun	30 min 2 hills	XT or 20 min of easy running	off	6 x 1 mi (marathon speed)
C Plan	off	30-45 min 4CD 4Acg 3 x 1 mi (marathon pace)	off/XT	30-35 min 4CD 4Acg	45-60 min 2 hills	off	6 x 1 mi (marathon speed)

1. "B" & "C" runners will be doing one mile repeats on the weekend. These should be run 30 seconds per mile faster than goal marathon pace. Walk for 5 minutes between each. You can use the same run-walk-run ratio you plan to use in the race itself, or cut the walk break slightly.

2. On the Tuesday and the Saturday mile repeat workouts, try to get into a "groove" so that you are running smoothly at the pace assigned. Ease into the walk break, and then ease out of the walk break.

3. Try to run as close as possible to the pace assigned, on each mile repeat. This is how you learn pace judgement.

4. Look back over your journal for the last 4 weeks of training for problems. Then look ahead and make notes so that you can avoid those problems.

Week # 35

	Mon	Tues	Wed	Thurs	Fri	Sat	Sun
A Plan	off	30 min 4CD 4Acg	off	30 min 0 hills	off	off	16-17 miles
B Plan	off	30 min 4CD 4Acg 3 x 1 mi (marathon pace)	off/XT H₂Orun	30 min 2 hills	XT or 20 min of easy running	off	8 x 1 mi (marathon speed)
C Plan	off	30-45 min 4CD 4Acg 3 x 1 mi (marathon pace)	off/XT H₂Orun	30-35 min 4CD 4Acg	45-60 min 2 hills	off	8 x 1 mi (marathon speed)

1. Take an extra 2-3 days off from running at the first sign of injury: Inflammation, loss of function, or pain that does not go away with extended walking.

2. Read the mental toughness section of this book, and use the "magic words" techniques during your mile repeats.

3. The day before and after long runs, and mile repeats, drink about 4-8 oz of electrolyte beverage like Accelerade, about every 1-2 hours throughout the day. This will help to "top off" your fluid levels and your electrolyte levels.

4. During your mile repeats, try to use your "gliding" technique, learned during the Acg drills. Even if you glide for only a few yards, you'll save resources.

	Mon	Tues	Wed	Thurs	Fri	Sat	Sun
A Plan	off	30 min 4CD 4Acg	off	30 min 2 hills	off	off	3-4 miles
B Plan	off	30 min 4CD 4cg	off/XT H₂Orun	30 min 0 hills	XT or 20 min of easy running	off	23 Miles
C Plan	off	30-45 min 4CD 4Acg	off/XT H₂Orun	30-35 min 0 hills 4Acg	45-60 min	off	23 miles

1. "A" runners should take it very easy this week. By letting the body rest up, you'll have more energy and motivation as you enter the final stage of the training.

2. Before the next long run, check to see if you are walking often enough on the long runs:

Note:

If your legs are cramping at the end of previous long runs, try walking more frequently and slowing the pace by 30-60 seconds per mile—from the beginning of the run.

9 min/mi—5-7 min run/1 min walk

9:30—4-1

10 to 11 min/mi—3-1

12 to 13 min/mi—2-1

14 to 15 min/mi—either 2-1 or 1-1

16 to 18 min/mi—1-1

19 to 21 min/mi—run 1 min/walk 2 min

3. You cannot run too slow on the long runs. The object is only to cover the distance. Enjoy these runs as you push back your endurance barriers.

4. You are making great progress! Think of how far you've come since the beginning of the year.

5. If you are experiencing low blood sugar at the end of your long ones (hunger, loss of focus and concentration, etc.) try taking the blood sugar booster food you use, more frequently.

6. If the temperature during your one mile repeats is above 75 degrees, you should take more walking between each. Pour water over your head, and wet your running top before each mile repeat. You can also break up the miles into 800s when it is too hot to maintain pace on the miles. Just aim to run twice the number of 800s and walk for 3 min between each.

	Mon	Tues	Wed	Thurs	Fri	Sat	Sun
A Plan	off	30 min 4CD 4Acg	off	30 min 0 hills	off	off	18-19 miles
B Plan	off	30 min 4CD 4Acg 3 x 1 mi (marathon pace)	off/XT H₂Orun	30 min 2 hills	XT or 20 min of easy running	off	10x 1 mi (marathon speed)
C Plan	off	30-45 min 4CD 4Acg 3 x 1 mi (marathon pace)	off/XT H₂Orun 4Acg	30-35 min 4CD	30 min 2 hills	off	10x 1 mi (marathon speed)

1. If you are struggling or slowing down at the end of your long runs or speed sessions, slow down the pace at the beginning of the next workouts.

2. Read through the "mental toughness" chapter in this book. These techniques have helped thousands to avoid listening to the negative messages that spew out of the left brain. For best results, you should try several of the techniques in this chapter on your long runs and speed sessions. Then, use the ones that work for you in the races.

3. Be sure to re-read the section on heat disease in this book, and comply. Remember that when the temperature reaches 60°F you need to slow down by 30 seconds a mile for every 5 degrees above this temperature—on long runs and races longer than 10K.

Week # 38

	Mon	Tues	Wed	Thurs	Fri	Sat	Sun
A Plan	off	30 min 4CD 4Acg	off	30 min 2 hills	off	off	3-4 miles
B Plan	off	30 min 4CD 4Acg 2 x 1 mi (marathon pace)	off/XT H$_2$Orun	30 min 2 hills	XT or 20 min of easy running	off	1 mi test (6 mi total)
C Plan	off	30-45 min 4CD 4Acg 2 x 1 mi (marathon pace)	off/XT H$_2$Orun	30-35 min 4CD 4Acg	45-60 min 2 hills	off	1 mi test (6 mi total)

1. Easy week! You have earned the right to take an easier week—in mileage. Except for the one mile test and the 2 x 1 marathon pace miles, the pace of the runs should be easy also.

2. Everyone has a few "bad days" or performance letdowns. Don't let these bother you unless you see a trend. If this occurs, look at the "trouble-shooting" section of this book, and make corrections.

3. Keep adjusting your pace on each lap of the one mile tests, so that you can run faster. Sometimes this means taking a little more walking at the end of the first or second lap. Even on one mile races, most runners record their fastest times when they run a negative split: the second half is faster than the first.

	Mon	Tues	Wed	Thurs	Fri	Sat	Sun
A Plan	off	30 min 4CD 4Acg	off	30 min 2 hills	off	off	1 mi test (4 mi total)
B Plan	off	30 min 4CD 4cg	off/XT H$_2$Orun	30 min 0 hills	XT	off	26 Miles
C Plan	off	30-45 min 4CD 4Acg	off/XT H$_2$Orun	30-35 min 4CD 4Acg	30 min 0 hills	off	26 miles

1. "B" and "C" plan folks are running a long training run of marathon distance this weekend. Before this run, do another "reality check on your long run pace:

   - average your last 3 one mile tests
   - multiply the time by 1.3
   - add 2 minutes to this

   Example: 10 minutes in the one mile test equals a hard marathon of 13 min/mi. Long run pace should be 15 min/mi.

2. Be sure to correct for temperature increase above 60F (add 30 sec/mi for every 5 degrees of temp increase).

3. Fluid intake on long runs should average about 4-6 oz, every mile to two miles.

4. If you are cramping at the end of long runs, increase the frequency of the walk breaks at the beginning of all future runs.

	Mon	Tues	Wed	Thurs	Fri	Sat	Sun
A Plan	off	30 min 4CD 4Acg	off	30 min 0 hills	off	off	20-21 miles
B Plan	off	30 min 4CD 4Acg 2 x 1 mi (marathon pace)	off/XT H$_2$Orun	30 min 2 hills	XT or 20 min of easy running	off	8 miles easy
C Plan	off	30-45 min 4CD 4Acg 2 x 1 mi (marathon pace)	off/XT H$_2$Orun	30-35 min 4CD 4Acg	45 min 2 hills	off	8 miles easy

1. Make sure that you're taking the walk breaks you need on the long runs. Even if you can run farther between walk breaks, it's best to take them as suggested. This will speed up recovery.

2. "B" and "C" runners should take walk breaks on the mile repeats, approximately as you plan to take the breaks in the marathon itself.

3. On long runs make sure that you are running at least 2 min/mi slower than your mile tests are predicting. Slower long runs reduce injury risk, while they speed up the healing.

4. "B" and "C" runners will have an easy week. Run very slowly on all runs except the 2 x 1 mile on Tuesday.

Week # 41

	Mon	Tues	Wed	Thurs	Fri	Sat	Sun
A Plan	off	30 min 4CD 4Acg	off H₂Orun	30 min 2 hills	off	off	4-5 miles
B Plan	off	30 min 4CD 4Acg 2 x 1 mi (marathon pace)	off/XT H₂Orun	30 min 0 hills	XT or 20 min of easy running	off	12x1 mi (Marathon speed)
C Plan	off	30-45 min 4CD 4Acg 2 x 1 mi (marathon pace)	off/XT	30-35 min 4CD 4Acg	30 min 0 hills	off	12x1 mi (Marathon speed)

1. "A" runners: Easy Week! Run slowly on practically every run to let any tired muscles rest.
2. You have encountered most (if not all) of the negative messages you can get from your left brain. As you rehearse getting these, you will desensitize yourself to them. This will allow you to keep on running when you receive them in the goal race
3. If you are still getting a lot of negative messages at the end of your long runs, read the mental toughness section—especially the part designated as "dirty tricks"

Week # 42

	Mon	Tues	Wed	Thurs	Fri	Sat	Sun
A Plan	off	30 min 4CD 4Acg	off	30 min 2 hills	off	off	1 mi test (6 mi total)
B Plan	off	30 min 4CD 4Acg 2 x 1 mi (marathon pace)	off/XT H₂Orun	30 min 2 hills	XT or 20 min of easy running	off	1 mi test (8 mi total)
C Plan	off	30-45 min 4CD 4Acg 2 x 1 mi (marathon pace)	off/XT H₂Orun	30-35 min 4CD 4Acg	45-60 min 2 hills	off	1 mi test (8 mi total)

1. EASY Week! Run slowly on almost every run (except for the mile test)

2. After this one mile test, look back at the trend of times in this test. If you are slowing down during the last two laps, you should run more easily during the first part of your workouts and your long runs.

Week # 43

	Mon	Tues	Wed	Thurs	Fri	Sat	Sun
A Plan	off	30 min 4CD 4Acg	off	30 min 0 hills	off	off	22-23 miles
B Plan	off	30 min 4CD 4cg	off/XT H₂Orun	30 min 0 hills	XT or 20 min of easy running	off	29 Miles
C Plan	off	30-45 min 4CD 4Acg	off/XT H₂Orun	30-35 min 4CD 4Acg	30 min 0 hills	off	29 miles

1. On this long run, run 2:30 to 4 minutes slower than current predicted marathon race pace (one mile test average x 1.3). It would also help to take walk breaks more frequently. For example, if you have been using a 4-1 ratio, drop down to 3-1 or 2-1. There is no downside to this.

2. Be sure to make the adjustment for increase in temperature: slow down by 30 sec a mile for every 5 degrees above 60°F.

3. It is natural to feel really tired during the latter 3 miles of these longer long runs. A slower starting pace, with more liberal walks will reduce or eliminate this—while giving all of the benefits.

4. Read the mental toughness chapter the night before the 29 miler. This run will push back your endurance barriers!

5. Endurox Excel pills, taken an hour before the start of a long or hard run, have been shown in research to speed recovery.

Week # 44

	Mon	Tues	Wed	Thurs	Fri	Sat	Sun
A Plan	off	30 min 4CD 4Acg	off	30 min 2 hills	off	off	4-6 miles
B Plan	off	30 min 4CD 4Acg	off/XT H₂Orun	30 min 2 hills	XT or 20 min of easy running	off	4x 1 mi (marathon speed) (7 miles total for the day)
C Plan	off	30-45 min 4CD 4Acg	off/XT H₂Orun	30-35 min 4CD 4Acg	30 min 2 hills	off	4x 1 mi (marathon speed) (7 miles total for the day)

1. This will be another easy week.

2. Look at the schedule for the weeks after the marathon. Note that there are social runs, scenic runs, etc. Now is a good time to set these up and write them on your appointment calendar or training journal. These fun runs will keep you motivated during the weeks after the marathon.

3. It's not too early to think of your next goal beyond the marathon. Get a new training journal and start penciling in key races or goals and you will be setting up your next one year plan.

4. In between the mile repeats (B & C runners) walk for 6 min or more. If you are struggling after the 29 miler, just jog for 7 miles with lots of walking.

Week # 45

	Mon	Tues	Wed	Thurs	Fri	Sat	Sun
A Plan	off	30 min 4CD 4Acg	off H₂Orun	30 min 2 hills	off	off	1 mile test (7 miles total)
B Plan	off	30 min 4CD 4Acg 2 x 1 mi (marathon pace)	off/XT H₂Orun	30 min 2 hills	XT or 20 min of easy running	off	13x1 mi (Marathon speed)
C Plan	off	30-45 min 4CD 4Acg 2x1mi (mar pace)	off/XT	30-35 min 4CD 4Acg	30 min	off	14x1 mi (Marathon speed) 0 hills

1. Easy Week! Run slowly on practically every run to let any tired muscles rest.

2. In this last mile repeat workout (B & C runners), run the first 4 of them 20 seconds faster than goal pace. If you are feeling good, run the rest of the repeats at 30 sec faster than goal pace. Walk for 6 min between each one.

3. Endurox R4, taken within 30 min of the finish of a hard or long run, has great results in speeding up recovery.

4. You have encountered most (if not all) of the negative messages you can get from your left brain. As you rehearse getting these, you will desensitize yourself to them. This will allow you to keep on running when you receive them in the goal race.

5. If you are still getting a lot of negative messages at the end of your long runs, read the mental toughness section—especially the part designated as "dirty tricks"

Week # 46

	Mon	Tues	Wed	Thurs	Fri	Sat	Sun
A Plan	off	30 min 4CD 4Acg	off	30 min 0 hills	off	off	24-26 miles
B Plan	off	30 min 4CD 4Acg 2 x 1 mi (mar. pace)	off/XT H$_2$Orun	30 min 2-4 hills	XT or walk	off	1 mi test (8 mi total)
C Plan	off	30-45 min 4CD 4Acg 2 x 1 mi (mar. pace)	off/XT H$_2$Orun	30-35 min 4CD 4Acg	30-40 min 2-4 hills	off	1 mi test (8 mi total)

1. Look back at your last 4 one mile tests. Adjust your pace and walk breaks during the test this week so that you learn from your past mistakes and are picking up speed during the last 2 laps on this one.

2. After this test, take the last 4 one mile tests, toss out the slowest, and average them. Multiply by 1.3. This is your predicted finishing pace (per mile) for the marathon. Here is an example of your pacing strategy for the marathon—assuming 60F or cooler.

Avg on one mile tests: 10 min

X 1.3 = 13 min pace in the marathon

First 6 miles: 13:10-13:20 ea (1-1 or 2-1)

Miles 7-20: 13 min per mile (2-1)

Miles 21-26: whatever you want!

	Mon	Tues	Wed	Thurs	Fri	Sat	Sun
A Plan	off	30 min 4CD 4Acg	off	30 min 0 hills	off	off	4-6 miles
B Plan	off	30 min 4CD 4cg 1 x 1 mi (m-p)	off/XT	30 min 0 hills	XT	off	Marathon Goal Race or walk
C Plan	off	30 min 4CD 4Acg 1x1 mi (m-p)	off/XT	30 min 4CD 4Acg	30 min 0 hills	off	Marathon Goal Race

1. There is nothing you can do to improve your marathon time between now and starting time. Run easy leading up to the weekend. Walk around a little the day before the race—but not too much.

2. Remember that whatever you save up in the first half of the run, will be available to you during the last 6 miles of the marathon.

3. You can do it!

Week # 48

	Mon	Tues	Wed	Thurs	Fri	Sat	Sun
A Plan	off	30 min 4CD 4Acg	off	30 min 2 hills	off	off	1 mile test
B Plan	off	20 min	off/XT	20 min 0 hills	XT or walk	off	4-6 miles
C Plan	off	20 min	off/XT	20 min	20 min	off	4-6 miles

1. "B" & "C" runners: Recovery week—take every run easy, with lots of walking.

2. "A" Enjoy the glow of your long run the previous weekend—you've earned this.

Week # 49

	Mon	Tues	Wed	Thurs	Fri	Sat	Sun
A Plan	off	30 min 2CD 2Acg	off	30 min 0 hills	off	off	Marathon Goal Race
B Plan	off	30 min 4CD 4Acg	off/XT	30 min 1 hill	XT or walk	off	6-8 miles (social run)
C Plan	off	30-45 min 4CD 4Acg	off/XT	30-35 min 1 hill	20 min	off	6-8 miles (social run)

1. Take as much walking as you wish on all runs.

2. Enjoy every run!

Week # 50

	Mon	Tues	Wed	Thurs	Fri	Sat	Sun
A Plan	off	20 min	off	20 min 0 hills	off	off	4-6 miles
B Plan	off	30 min 4CD 4Acg	off/XT	30 min 2 hills	XT or 20 min	off	10-12 miles scenic
C Plan	off	30-45 min 4CD 4Acg	off/XT	30-35 min 2 hills	30-45 min	off	10-12 miles Scenic

1. Congratulations! Only one-tenth of one percent of the population finishes a marathon each year. You are part of an elite group.

Week # 51

	Mon	Tues	Wed	Thurs	Fri	Sat	Sun
A Plan	off	20 min 2CD 2Acg	off	20 min 1 hill	off	off	6-8 miles
B Plan	off	30 min 4CD 4Acg	off/XT	30 min 3 hills	XT or 20 min	off	5 mi or fun race
C Plan	off	30-45 min 4CD 4Acg	off/XT	30-35 min 3 hills	45 min	off	5 mi or fun race

1. While "B" and "C" runners should be recovered it is not a good idea to run an all-out race. Pace a friend who runs slower than you do. Enjoy the festivities.

2. You should have your next one year plan started by now. Pencil in more of the blank spaces.

Week # 52

	Mon	Tues	Wed	Thurs	Fri	Sat	Sun
A Plan	off	20 min 4CD 4Acg	off	20 min 2 hills	off	off	6-12 miles
B Plan	off	30 min 4CD 4Acg	off/XT	30-35 min 4 hills	XT or 20 min of easy running	off	10-12 mi (scenic run) (or social)
C Plan	off	30-45 min 4CD 4Acg	off/XT	30-35 min	30-45 min 4 hills	off	10-12 mi (scenic run) (or social)

1. As you complete the 52 week plan, you should be preparing for the next one. It is always better to keep the momentum going—rather than stop running completely. Find the right mix of running days and off days that works for you.

2. Go through your training journal and make notes. During the next year, make the changes that will improve your running and make it more enjoyable.

Congratulations on completing your year round plan!

MAKING

ADJUSTMENTS

Almost everyone has interruptions and schedule problems. By using your journal to schedule your workouts, you can make the changes you need, and stay on track for your goals. Even more important is the ability to go back through the past, locate problems, and make changes in the future.

Here are some of the solutions to common problems:

Race weekend doesn't match up with the 52 week plan

The best solution is to eliminate the week after the long run on the last two cycles (B & C runners) to make a 3 week cycle. Or, (for all runners) once the long run reaches 20 miles, you may go to 4 weeks between long runs by inserting an easy week.

Injury interruption

Top priority is to let the injury heal to the point that you can continue with training. Most injuries allow for easy running before compete healing has occurred. When you have questions about this, talk to your doctor.

Speedwork puts a much greater stress on a weak link. Before restarting your speed training, you need the best advice possible from your medical team. Even then, you will need to start back conservatively:

1. When given clearance to start back, run a very easy running week or two to get your legs, tendons, etc. working together again.

2. When given clearance, and the injured area seems ready, do a "test speed workout". Warm up thoroughly and then run only 2-3 repetitions, running each slower than you were running before the injury, with more rest than you would usually take.

3. If there are no problems from this test, then ease back into the training on the schedule.

4. Most injury interruptions will take 2-3 weeks of transition to get you back on the 52 week plan. If you had more than 10 days off from running, it may take more time to get back on plan.

5. Use your journal to add weeks to the plan.

6. Be sensitive to your "weak link" that was injured.

Sickness interruption

Top priority is to ensure that you are not going to pull your resistance further down by returning to running. If there is a lung infection, don't run, and get full clearance from your doctor before starting back. Lung infections will also have a longer term effect on your strength, requiring more time to transition back to running. When you and the doctor feel that you can resume training, ease back as follows:

1. Run a very easy running week or two, with liberal walk breaks, to get legs, tendons, etc. working together again.

2. When given medical clearance for speedwork, and you feel up to it, do a "test speed workout". Warm up

thoroughly and then run only 2-3 repetitions, running each slower than you were running before the sickness, with more rest than you would usually take between each.

3. If there are no problems from this test, then ease back into the training on the schedule.

4. Most sickness interruptions will take only 1-2 weeks of transition to get back to the 52 week plan.

5. Use your journal to add weeks to your plan.

6. Be sensitive to any signs that you may be lowering your resistance or getting another infection.

Career, vacation, family interruptions

Life will intervene several times during a year. When you did not have a sickness or injury, you need little transition time to resume the plan. It will help greatly on these "vacation from your plan" weeks to do at least 15 minutes of running, every other day. This will maintain most of your running adaptations.

YOUR JOURNAL —YOUR PLANNING AND EVALUATION TOOL

This is your book

Yes, you are writing a book. You already have the outline: your 52 week plan. As you follow it, you document the good times, and the slow ones. The journal will allow you to modify your plan and track the changes. Later, you can look back after success or disappointments and often find reasons for either. If we don't look at our negative running history, we will have a tendency to repeat it.

Example of a training journal:

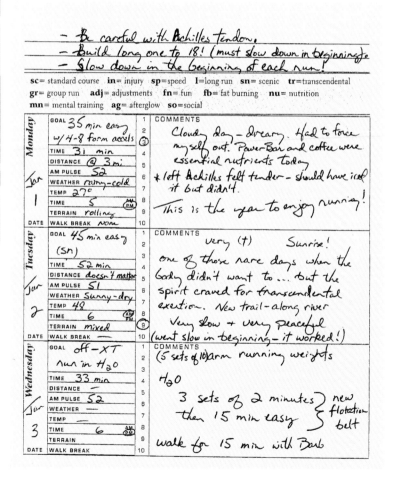

- Be careful with Achilles tendon.
- Build long one to 18! (must slow down in beginning)
- Slow down in the beginning of each run!

sc= standard course **in**= injury **sp**=speed **l**=long run **sn**= scenic **tr**=transcendental
gr= group run **adj**= adjustments **fn**= fun **fb**= fat burning **nu**= nutrition
mn= mental training **ag**= afterglow **so**=social

Monday
GOAL 35 min easy w/4-8 form accels
TIME 31 min
DISTANCE @ 3 mi.
AM PULSE 52
WEATHER rainy-cold
TEMP 27°
TIME 5
TERRAIN rolling
WALK BREAK none

COMMENTS
Cloudy day - dreary. Had to force myself out. PowerBar and coffee were essential nutrients today
* left Achilles felt tender - should have iced it but didn't.
This is the year to enjoy running!

Tuesday
GOAL 45 min easy (sn)
TIME 52 min
DISTANCE doesn't matter
AM PULSE 51
WEATHER Sunny-dry
TEMP 48
TIME 6
TERRAIN mixed
WALK BREAK

COMMENTS
very (t)   Sunrise!
one of those rare days when the body didn't want to ... but the spirit craved for transcendental exertion. New trail - along river
Very slow + very peaceful
(went slow in beginning - it worked!)

Wednesday
GOAL off - XT run in H₂O
TIME 33 min
DISTANCE —
AM PULSE 52
WEATHER —
TEMP —
TIME 6
TERRAIN
WALK BREAK

COMMENTS
(5 sets of 10 arm running weights
H₂O
3 sets of 2 minutes } new
then 15 min easy } flotation belt
walk for 15 min with Barb

The various types of journals

Calendar—facing you on the wall

Many runners start recording their runs on a wall calendar—or one that is posted on the refrigerator. Looking at the miles recorded is empowering. But equally motivating for many is seeing too many "zeros" on days that should have been running days. If you're not sure whether you will really get into this journal process, you may find it easiest to start with a calendar.

Week of | Jan 1

Thursday / Jan 4
GOAL: 35 min easy (sc)
TIME: 45 min
DISTANCE @ 6.5
AM PULSE: 49
WEATHER: Cloudy
TEMP: 40°
TIME: 6 PM
TERRAIN: rolling
WALK BREAK: —

COMMENTS:
Great run with Barb, Wes + Sambo — who took out the pace too fast + died at the end. The rest of us caught up on the gossip. Achilles ached so I iced it for 15 minutes.

Friday / Jan 5
GOAL: 45 min (sp) 5 × 800 meter
TIME: 1:15
DISTANCE: 7.5 mi
AM PULSE: 53
WEATHER: 45°
TEMP: Sunny
TIME: 5 PM
TERRAIN: track
WALK BREAK: 400 m

COMMENTS:
2:30
2:36
2:33 left
2:37
2:32 return
2:36
12 min warm up and warm down
My best workout in years!
- walked 400 m between each
- struggled on last one
Achilles ached - iced 15 min

Saturday / Jan 6
GOAL: Off
TIME:
DISTANCE:
AM PULSE: 55
WEATHER:
TEMP:
TIME: AM PM
TERRAIN:
WALK BREAK:

COMMENTS:
Kids soccer (Mom)
* Westin scores goal bouncing off his back
1st goal of season!
Brennan's cross country (aft) Invitational
* Brennan comes from 8th to 3rd in the last half mile. I'm so proud!

Sunday / Jan 7
GOAL: 18 mi (l) easy!
TIME: 2:53
DISTANCE: 18 mi
AM PULSE: 52
WEATHER: 50°
TEMP: dry no wind
TIME: PM
TERRAIN: flat
WALK BREAK: 1 min/mi

COMMENTS:
It was great to cover 18 miles—wish I had a group
longest run in 18 months!
but...
* went too fast in the first 5 miles
* Achilles hurt afterward - take 3 days off
* Power Bar + water from 10 mi kept spirits up

* Pulse is up - I'm not recovering - need more days off/week

An organized running journal

When you use a product that is designed for running, you don't have to think to record the facts. The spaces on the page ask you for certain info, and you will learn to fill it very quickly. This leaves you time to use some of the open space for the creative thoughts and ideas that pop out during a run. Look at the various journals available and pick one that looks to be easier to use, and to carry with you. I've included a sample page of my **Jeff Galloway Training Journal** as one example.

Notebook

You don't need to have a commercial product. You can create your own journal by using a basic school notebook, of your choice. Find one of the size that works best with your lifestyle (briefcase, purse, etc.) Below you will find the items that I've found helpful for most runners to record. But the best journals are those that make it easier for you to collect the data you find interesting, while allowing for creativity. The non-limiting nature of a notebook is a more comfortable format for runners that like to write a lot one day, and not so much another day.

Computer logs

There are a growing number of software products that allow you to sort through information more quickly. In working with a company (PC Coach) to incorporate my training program, I discovered that this format speeds up the search for needed information. As you set up your own codes and sections you can pick data that is important to you, sort it to see trends, and plan ahead. Some software (including mine) allows for you to download data from a heart monitor or GPS watch.

The planning process

1. Look over the 52 week plan and make any changes needed to customize it for your use.

2. Write down the goal races, on the appropriate weeks in your journal. Take a hi-lighter or other method to make these weeks stand out.

3. Write down the assigned workouts, for each day of each week for the next 8 weeks—in pencil.

4. Look at each of the next 8 weeks quickly to make sure you don't have any trips, meetings, family responsibilities that require adjusting the workouts.

5. Each week, add another week's workouts in pencil, and note any changes in your travel, etc. schedule.

6. Each week, look ahead carefully at the next two weeks to ensure that the workouts are adjusted to your real life schedule.

The data recording

1. As soon as you can after a run, write what you did in your journal:
   - mileage
   - pace
   - repetitions—times
   - rest interval
   - aches or pains
   - problems

In addition, you may also record:

- Time of run:
- Total Time running:
- Weather:
- Temp____
- Precipitation____
- Humidity____
- Walk-Run frequency
- Any special segments of the run (speed, hills, race, etc.)
- Running companion
- Terrain
- How did you feel (1-10)
- Comments:

2. Go back over the list again and fill in more details—emotional responses, changes in energy or blood sugar level, and location of places where you had aches and pains—even if they went away during the run. You are looking for patterns of items that could indicate injury, blood sugar problems, lingering fatigue, etc.

2. Helpful additions (usually in a blank section at the bottom of the page)
   - Improvement Thoughts
   - Things I should have done differently
   - Interesting Happenings
   - Funny things
   - Strange things
   - Stories, right brain crazy thoughts

Your morning pulse is a great guide of overstress

Recording morning pulse—immediately upon waking

1. As soon as you are conscious—but before you have thought much about anything—count your pulse rate for a minute. Record it before you forget it. If you don't have your journal by your bed, then keep a piece of paper handy—with a pen.

2. It is natural for there to be some fluctuations, based upon the time you wake up, how long you have been awake, etc. But after several weeks and months, these will balance themselves out. The ideal would be to catch the pulse at the instant that you are awake, before the shock of an alarm clock, thoughts of work stress, etc.

3. After 2 weeks or so of readings, you can establish a base line morning pulse. Take out the top 2 high readings and then average the readings.

4. The average is your guide. If the rate is 5% higher than your average, take an easy day. When the rate is 10% higher, and there is no reason for this (you woke up from an exciting dream, medication, infection, etc.) then your muscles may be tired indeed. Take the day off if you have a walk-run scheduled for that day.

5. If your pulse stays high for more than a week, call your doctor to see if there is a reason for this (medication, hormones, metabolic changes, etc.).

THE DRILLS—

TO MAKE RUNNING FASTER AND EASIER

The following drills have helped thousands of runners run more efficiently and faster. Each one develops different capabilities, and each rewards the individual for running smoother, reducing impact, using momentum, and increasing the cadence or turnover of feet and legs. With each drill, you'll be teaching yourself to move more more directly and easily down the road.

When?

These should be done on a non-long run day. It is fine, however, to do them as part of your warm-up, before a race or a speed workout. Many runners have also told me that the drills are a nice way to break up an average run that otherwise might be called "boring."

Cadence or turnover drill

This is an easy drill that makes your running form smoother and easier. By doing it regularly, you pull all the elements of good running form together at the same time. One drill a week will help you step lightly, increasing the number of steps you take per minute. This will help you run faster, with less effort.

1. Warm up by walking for 5 minutes, and running and walking very gently for 10 minutes.
2. Start jogging slowly for 1-2 minutes, and then time yourself for 30 seconds. During this half minute, count the number of times your left foot touches.
3. Walk around for a minute or so.
4. On the 2nd—30 second drill, increase the count by 1 or 2.
5. Repeat this 3-7 more times. Each time trying to increase by 1-2 additional counts.

In the process of improving turnover, the body's internal monitoring system, coordinates a series of adaptations which makes the feet, legs, nerve system and timing mechanism work together as an efficient team:

- Your foot touches more gently

- Extra, inefficient motions of the foot and leg are reduced or eliminated

- Less effort is spent on pushing up or moving forward

- You stay lower to the ground

- The ankle becomes more efficient

- Ache and pain areas are not overused

Acceleration-glider drills

This drill is a very easy and gentle form of speed play, or fartlek. By doing it regularly, you develop a range of speeds, with the muscle conditioning to move smoothly from one to the next. The greatest benefit comes as you learn how to "glide," or coast off your momentum.

1. Done on a non-long-run day, in the middle of a shorter run, or as a warm-up for a speed session or a race—or test day.
2. Warm up with at least half a mile of easy running.
3. Many runners do the turnover drill just after the easy warm-up, and then do the acceleration-gliders. But these can be done separately from the turnover drill, if desired.
4. Run 4-8 of them.
5. Do this at least once a week.
6. No sprinting—never run all-out.

After teaching this drill at my one-day running schools and weekend retreats for years, I can say that most people learn better through practice when they work on the concepts listed below—rather than the details—of the drill. So just get out there and try them!

Gliding—The most important concept. This is like coasting off the momentum of a downhill run. You can do some of your gliders running down a hill if you want, but it is important to do at least two of them on the flat land.

Do this every week—As in the turnover drills, the regularity of the drill is very important. If you're like most runners, you won't glide very far at first. Regular practice will help you glide farther and farther.

Don't sweat the small stuff—I've included a general guideline of how many steps to do with each part of the drill, but don't worry about getting any set number of steps. It's best to get into a flow with this drill and not worry at all about how many steps you are taking.

Smooth transition—between each of the components. Each time you "shift gears" you are using the momentum of the current mode to start you into the next mode. Don't make a sudden and abrupt change, but have a smooth transition between modes.

Here's how it's done:

- Start by jogging very slowly for about 15 steps.
- Then, jog faster for about 15 steps—increasing to a regular running pace for you.

- Now, over the next about fifteen steps, gradually increase the speed to your current race pace.
- OK, it's time to glide, or coast. Allow yourself to gradually slow down to a jog using momentum as long as you can. At first you may only glide for 4 or 5 steps. As the months go by you will get up to 20, then 30 and beyond....you're gliding!

Overall Purpose: As you do this drill, every week, your form will become smoother at each mode of running. Congratulations! You are learning how to keep moving at a fairly fast pace without using much energy. This is the main object of the drill.

There will be some weeks when you will glide longer than others—don't worry about this. By doing this drill regularly, you will find yourself coasting or gliding down the smallest of inclines, and even for 10-20 yards on the flat, on a regular basis. Gliding conserves energy—reduces soreness, fatigue, and maintains a faster pace in races.

THE PRINCIPLES
GREAT RUNNING

OF
FORM

After having analyzed over 10 thousand runners, in my running schools and weekend retreats, I've found that most runners are running very close to their ideal efficiency. The mistakes are seldom big ones. But a series of small mistakes can slow you down or create major aches, pains and sometimes injuries. By making a few minor adjustments, most runners can feel better and run faster.

Faster runners tend to make mistakes that cost them seconds and sometimes minutes in races. Before I detail these common problems, let's look at some principles of running form for distances longer than 200 meters (half a lap around a track).

I believe that running is an inertia activity

This means that your primary mission is to maintain your momentum. Very little strength is needed to run—even to run fast for short races like the 800 meters. During the first hundred meters you'll get your body into the motion and rhythm for your run. After that, the best strategy is to conserve energy while maintaining that forward inertia. To reduce fatigue, aches and pains, your right brain, helped by muscle memory, intuitively fine-tunes your mechanics and motion to minimize effort.

Humans have many bio-mechanical adaptations working for them, which have been made more efficient over more than a million years of walking and running. The anatomical running efficiency of the human body originates in the ankle and achilles tendon—which I treat as a unit. This is no average body part, however, but an extremely sophisticated system of levers, springs, balancing devices, and more. Bio-mechanics experts believe that this degree of development was not needed for walking. When our ancient ancestors had to run to survive, the ankle/achilles adapted to endurance running/walking producing a masterpiece of bio-engineering.

Through a series of speed sessions and drills, you can maximize use of the achilles and ankle so that a very little amount of muscle work produces a quicker, consistent forward movement. During the first few speed sessions your legs may be a little sore. But as you get in better and better shape, with improved endurance, you'll find yourself going farther and faster with little or no increased effort. Other muscle groups offer support and help to fine-tune the process. When you feel aches and pains that might be due to the way you run, going back to the minimal use of the ankle and achilles tendon can often leave you feeling smooth and efficient very quickly.

Three negative results of inefficient form:

1. Fatigue from extraneous motions becomes so severe that it takes much longer to recover.
2. Muscles or tendons are pushed so far beyond their limits that they break down and become injured—or just hurt.
3. The experience is so negative, that the desire to run is reduced, producing burnout.

Wobbling: It all starts with general fatigue that stresses your weak links. For example, if your knee gets weakened at the end of a workout or a race, and you keep pushing to maintain pace, your body will use other muscles and tendons to keep you going. You start to "wobble" as these alternatives are not designed to do the job. The longer you "wobble" the more prone to injury.

Stride extension when tired: There are several instincts that can hurt us. When tired, for example, many runners try to extend stride length to maintain pace. This may work for a while—at the expense of the quads, hamstrings, and several other components that are over-stressed. It is always better, when you feel even a slight aggravation at the end of a run, to cut stride, and get back into a smooth motion. It's OK to push through tiredness when running smoothly as long as you are not feeling pain in any area. But if this means extending stride or wobbling (which aggravates your weak links) it's not OK.

Be sensitive and avoid irritation: I don't suggest that everyone should try to create perfect form. But when you become aware of your form problems, and make changes to keep them from producing aches and pains, you'll run smoother, reduce fatigue, and run faster, on that day.

Relaxed muscles—especially at the end of the run

Overall, the running motion should feel smooth, and there should be no tension in your neck, back, shoulders or legs. Even during the last half mile of a hard workout or race, try to maintain the three main elements of good form, and you'll stay relaxed: upright posture, feet low to the ground, and relaxed stride. You should not try to push through tightness and pain. Adjust your form to reduce aches and recovery time.

The big three: posture, stride, and bounce

In thousands of individual running form consultations, I've discovered that when runners have problems, they tend to occur in these three areas. Often the problems are like a signature—tending to be very specific to the areas that you overuse, because of your unique movement patterns. By making a few small changes in your running form, you can reduce or eliminate the source of the problems—the source of the pain.

I. Posture

Good running posture is actually good body posture. The head is naturally balanced over the shoulders, which are aligned over the hips. As the foot comes underneath, all of these elements are in balance so that no energy is needed to prop up the body. You shouldn't have to work to pull a wayward body back from a wobble or inefficient motion.

Forward lean—the most common mistake

The posture errors tend to be mostly due to a forward lean—especially when we are tired. The head wants to get to the finish as soon as possible, but the legs can't go any faster. A common tendency at the end of a speed session is to lean with the head. In races, this results in more than a few falls around the finish line. A forward lean will often concentrate fatigue, soreness and tightness in the lower back, or neck. Bio-mechanics experts note that a forward lean will reduce stride length, causing a slowdown or an increase in effort.

It all starts with the head. When the neck muscles are relaxed, the head can naturally seek an alignment that is naturally balanced on the shoulders. If there is tension in the neck, or soreness afterward, the head is usually leaning too far forward. This triggers a more general upper body imbalance in which the head and chest are suspended slightly ahead of the hips and feet. Sometimes, headaches result from this postural problem. Ask a running companion to tell you if and when your head is too far forward, or leaning down. This usually occurs at the end of a tiring run. The ideal position of the head is mostly upright, with your eyes focused about 30-40 yards ahead of you.

Sitting back

The hips are the other major postural component that can easily get out of alignment. A runner with this problem, when observed from the side, will have the butt behind the rest of the body. When the pelvis area is shifted back, the legs are not allowed to go through their ideal range of motion, and the stride length is shortened. This produces a slower pace, even when spending significant effort. Many runners tend to hit harder on their heels when their hips are shifted back—but this is not always the case.

A backward lean is rare

It is rare for runners to lean back, but it happens. In my experience, this is usually due to a structural problem in the spine or hips. If you do this, and you're having pain in the neck, back or hips, you should see an orthopedist that specializes in the back. One symptom is excessive shoe wear on the back of the heel—but there are other reasons why you may show this kind of wear.

Correction: "Puppet on a string"

The best correction I've found to postural problems has been this mental image exercise: imagine that you are a puppet on a string. In other words, you're suspended from above like a puppet—from the head and each side of the shoulders. In this way, your head lines up above the shoulders, the hips come directly underneath, and the feet naturally touch lightly—directly underneath. It won't hurt anyone to do the "puppet" several times during a run.

It helps to combine this image with a deep breath. About every 4-5 minutes, as you start to run after a walk break for example, take a deep, lower lung breath, straighten up and say "I'm a puppet." Then imagine that you don't have to spend energy maintaining this upright posture, because the strings attached from above keep you on track. As you continue to do this, you reinforce good posture, and the behavior can become a good habit.

Upright posture not only allows you to stay relaxed, you will probably improve stride length. When you lean forward, you'll be cutting your stride to stay balanced. When you straighten up, you'll receive a stride bonus of an inch or so, without any increase in energy. Note: don't try to increase stride length. When it happens naturally, you won't feel it—you'll just run faster.

An oxygen dividend

Breathing improves when you straighten up. A leaning body can't get ideal use out of the lower lungs. This can cause side pain. When you run upright the lower lungs can receive adequate air, maximize oxygen absorption, and reduce the chance of side pain.

II. Feet low to the ground

The most efficient stride is a shuffle—with feet right next to the ground. As long as you pick your foot up enough to avoid stumbling over a rock or uneven pavement, stay low to the ground. Most runners don't need to get more than 1" clearance—even when running fast. As you increase speed, and ankle action, you will come off the ground a bit more than this. Again, don't try to increase stride, let this happen naturally.

Your ankle combined with your achilles tendon will act as a spring, moving you forward on each running step. If you stay low to the ground, very little effort is required. Through this "shuffling" technique, running becomes almost automatic. When runners err on bounce, they try to push off too hard. This usually results in extra effort spent in lifting the body off the ground. You can think of this as energy wasted in the air—energy that could be used to run faster. The other negative force that penalizes a higher bounce is that of gravity. The higher you rise, the harder you fall. Each additional bounce off the ground delivers a lot more impact on feet and legs—which during speed sessions, races, and long runs, produces aches, pains and injuries.

The correction for too much bounce: Light touch

The ideal foot "touch" should be so light that you don't usually feel yourself pushing off or landing. This means that your foot stays low to the ground and goes though an efficient and natural motion. Instead of trying to overcome gravity, you get in synch with it. If your foot "slaps" when you run, you will definitely improve with a lighter touch.

Here's a "light touch drill":   During the middle of a run, time yourself for 20 seconds. Focus on one item: touching so softly that you don't hear your feet. Earplugs are not allowed for this drill. Imagine that you are running on thin ice or through a bed of hot coals. Do several of these 20 second touches, becoming quieter and quieter. You should feel very little impact on your feet as you do this drill.

III. Stride length

Studies have shown that as runners get faster, the stride length shortens. This clearly shows that the key to faster and more efficient running is increased cadence or quicker turnover of feet and legs. A major cause of aches, pains and injuries is a stride length that is too long. When in doubt, it is always better to err on the side of having a shorter stride.

Don't lift your knees!

Even most of the world class distance runners don't have a high knee lift. When your knees go too high, you are over-using the quadracep muscle (front of the thigh), resulting in a stride that is too long to be efficient. This often produces sore quads for the next day or two.

Don't kick out too far in front of you!

If you watch the natural movement of the leg, it will kick forward slightly as the foot gently moves forward in the running motion and then comes underneath to contact the ground. Let this be a natural motion that produces no tightness in the muscles behind the lower or upper leg.

Tightness in the front of the shin, or behind the knee, or in the hamstring (back of the thigh) are signs that you are kicking too far forward, and reaching out too far. Correct this by staying low to the ground, shortening the stride, and lightly touching the ground.

RACE DAY!

After having run in races, every year, since 1958, I've come to believe that success comes from getting the "little things" right. As you prepare for the big day, you will be organizing yourself, gaining mental focus, reducing tension, anticipating problems as you gear up to solve them. All of this sets yourself up for success.

In this chapter I will try to cover the most crucial areas that you will need on race day. Be sure to customize the proceedures based upon your needs, race venue, lifestyle, etc. Keep fine-tuning as you review. You should get more confident with each trip through the list.

Rehearsal

Use your speed workouts as "dress rehearsals" for your big day. Since you may be nervous, bring your checklists, and go through each item as you will do at the race itself. If at all possible, run on the race course several times. If you are running on a track in your "big test," work out on that track, if possible. You want to be familiar with every aspect of the environment surrounding the venue. Success may depend upon a feeling of confidence—that you own the venue. The more times you've been successful in workouts and runs at the track or race course, the more likely you'll feel this way.

If this is an important race that is out of town, it helps to run the course, and even stage a successful workout there. You'll learn the driving route, where to park (or which rapid transit station to exit), and what the site is like. If you will be driving, drive into the parking area several times to make sure you understand how to go exactly where you need to park. This will help you to feel at home with the staging area on race day—reducing raceday anxiety. If it's a road course, run over the last half mile of the course at least twice—the most important part of the course to know. It's also beneficial to do the first mile of the course to see which side of the road is best for walk breaks (location of sidewalks, etc.). If your goal race is on a track, visualize how you will be taking walk breaks, if you use them in the race.

Rehearse your line-up position. In a road race, you will be lining up in the area that corresponds with your pace. If you try to get ahead by starting too far forward, you could slow down runners that are faster. In your rehearsal you want to visualize getting to the side of the road before taking walk breaks. On a track you will be taking walk breaks to the outside.

What to look for in choosing a roadrace

- Fun and Festive—held in an interesting area, part of a town festival, music, expo with exhibits, etc.

- Well organized—the organizers...keep things organized: no long lines, easy to register, start goes off on time, water on the course, refreshments for all—even the slowest, no major problems

- Refreshments—some races have water, others have a buffet

- A good T-shirt or other reward—you'll wear it with pride

- The organizers focus on average or beginning runners

The afternoon before

Don't run the day before the race. You won't lose any conditioning if you take two days off from running leading up to the race. This is a personal issue and the number of days you do not run before a race is your choice. I recommend no more than two days of no running.

Some races require you to pick up your race number, and sometimes your computer chip (explained below) the day before. Look at the website or the entry form for instructions about this. Most races allow you to pick up your materials on race day—but be sure.

Race number

This is sometimes called a "bib number." It should be pinned on the front of the garment you'll be wearing when you cross the finish line. Ask your race organizing committee if you will have to wear a bib. If so, make sure you have 2-4 safety pins.

Computer chip

More and more races are using technology that automatically records your finish and split times along the course. You must wear a computer chip that is usually laced on the shoes, near the top. Some race result technology companies attach the chip to a velcro band around the ankle or arm. Read the instructions to make sure you are attaching this correctly. Be sure to turn this in after the race. The officials have volunteers to collect them, so stop and take them off your shoe, etc. right after the finish line. There is a steep fine ($) for those who don't turn in the chip.

The carbo loading dinner

Some races have a dinner the night before. At the dinner you will usually chat with runners at your table, and enjoy the evening. Don't eat much, however. Many runners assume, mistakenly, that they must eat a lot of food the night before. This is actually counterproductive. It takes at least 36 hours for most of the food you eat to be processed and useable in a race—usually longer. There is nothing you can eat the evening before a race that will help you.

But eating too much, or the wrong foods for you, can create a real problem. A lot of food in your gut, when you are bouncing up and down in a race, is stressful. A very common and embarrassing situation occurs when the gut is emptied to relieve this stress. While you don't want to starve yourself the afternoon and evening before, the best strategy is to eat small meals or snacks that you know are easy for the body to digest, and taper down the amount as you get closer to bed time. As always, it's best to have done a "rehearsal" of eating, so that you know what works, how much, when to stop eating, and what foods to avoid. The evening before your long morning runs is a good time to work on your eating plan so that you can replicate the successful routine leading up to raceday.

Drinking

The day before each goal race, drink when you are thirsty. If you haven't had a drink of water or sports drink in a couple of hours, drink half a cup to a cup (4-8 oz) each hour. Don't drink a lot of fluid during the morning of the race itself. This can lead to bathroom breaks before the race or the desire to do so during the race itself. Many races have porto-johns around the course, but some do not. This is another reason to preview the venue—and note the locations of bathrooms. It is a very common practice for runners that have consumed too much fluid that morning to find a tree or alley along the course. The best solution for most runners is to drink 6-10 oz of fluid about 2 hours before the race. Usually this is totally out of the system before the start.

Drinking Tip: If you practice drinking before your long runs, you can find the right amount of fluid that works best for you—on race day. Stage your drinks so that you know when you will be taking potty breaks, comfortably before the start of the race itself.

The night before

Eating is optional after 5pm. If you are hungry, have a light snack (or two) that you have tested before, and has not caused problems. Less is better, but don't go to bed hungry. Continue to have about 8oz of a good electrolyte beverage like Accelerade, over the 2 hours before you go to bed.

Alcohol is not recommended the night before, because the effects of this central nervous system depressant carry over to the next morning. Some runners have no trouble having one glass of wine or beer, while others are better off with none. If you decide to have a drink, I suggest that you make it one portion: 4-6 oz.

Pack your bag and lay out your clothes so that you don't have to think very much on race morning.

- Your watch, set up for the run-walk ratio you are using
- A pace chart, or wrist band, with lap times, or mile times
- Shoes
- Socks
- Shorts
- Top—see clothing thermometer in this book
- Pin race number on the front of the garment in which you will be finishing
- A few extra safety pins for your race number, or bib number
- Water, Accelerade, pre-race and post race beverages (such as Endurox R4), and a cooler if you wish
- Food for the drive in, and the drive home
- Bandages, skin lubricant, any other first aid items you may need
- Cash for registration if you are doing race day registration (check for exact amount, including late fee)
- $ 25-40 for gas, food, parking, etc
- Race chip attached according to the race instructions
- A few jokes or stories to provide laughs or entertainment before the start
- A copy of the "race day checklist", which is just below this section

Sleep

You may sleep well, or you may not. Don't worry if you don't sleep at all. Many runners I work with every year don't sleep a wink and have the best race of their lives. Of course, don't try to go sleepless....but if it happens, it is not a problem.

Race day checklist

Photocopy this list so that you will not only have a plan, you can carry it out in a methodical way. Pack the list in your race bag. Don't try anything new the day of your race—except for health or safety issues. The only item which has been successfully used for the first time in a race is walk breaks. Even first time users benefit significantly. Otherwise, stick with your plan.

Fluid and potty stops—after you wake up, drink 4-6 oz of water every half hour. If you have used a sports drink like Accelerade about 30 minutes before your runs, prepare it. Use a cooler if you wish. In order to avoid the bathroom stops, stop your fluid intake according to the timetable of what has worked for you before. For most, this is 2 hours before

Eat—what you have eaten before your harder runs. It is OK not to eat at all before a race of 10K or less unless you are a diabetic, then go with the plan that you and your doctor have worked out.

Get your bearings—walk around the site to find where you want to line up, and how you will get to the start. Choose a side of the road that has more shoulder or sidewalk for ease in taking walk breaks. If you are on a track, find a place where you can wait to line up, that makes you feel comfortable—this is your pre-race home.

Register or pick up your race number—If you already have all of your materials, you can bypass this step. If not, look at the signage in the registration area and get in the right line. Usually there is one for "race day registration" and one for those who registered online or in the mail and need to pick up their numbers.

Start your warm up 40-50 min before the start. If possible, go backwards on the course for about 0.5-0.6 mi and turn around. If this is a track race, run on the track if possible, and imagine yourself approaching the finish line with strength after each lap. This will give you a preview of the most important part of your race—the finish. Here is the warm-up routine:

- Walk for 5 minutes, slowly.

- Walk at a normal walking pace for 3-5 minutes, with a relaxed and short stride.

- Start your watch for the ratio of running and walking that you are using and do this, running and walking, for 10 minutes.

- Walk around for 5-10 minutes.

- Do 4-8 acceleration-gliders that gradually get you up to the speed you will be running in the race.

- If you have time, walk around the staging area, read your jokes, laugh, relax.

- Get in position and pick one side of the road or the other where you want to line up. If on a track, go to "your area" to wait for the start.

- When the road is closed, and runners are called onto the road, go to the curb and stay at the side of the road, near your preferred place. At the track, waiting for the start, visualize how you are going to start the race— comfortable and a bit conservative.

After the start

Remember that you can control how you feel during and afterward by conservative pacing and walks.

- Stick with your race plan and the run/walk ratio that has worked for you—take every walk break, especially the first one.

- Be conservative in pacing for the first one-third of the race and don't let yourself be pulled out too fast on the running portions.

- Stay with your plan. As people pass you, who are running faster than you or who are not taking walk breaks, tell yourself that you will catch them later—you will!

- If anyone interprets your walking as weakness, say: "This is my proven strategy for a strong finish."

- Even if you are pushing fairly hard, enjoy the race as much as possible, smile often.

- On warm days, pour water over your head at the start, possibly wetting your running top.

After mid-race

- When the going gets tough, do everything you can to relax, and keep the muscles resilient.

- Keep going—tell yourself this over and over during the tough moments. Shorten stride and pick up turnover.

- During the last half mile don't let your legs slow down. One more step! Success is not letting up. You can do it!

At the finish:

- In the upright position.

- With a smile on your face.

- Wanting to do it again.

After the finish

- Keep walking for at least a quarter of a mile.

- Drink about 4-8 oz of fluid.

- Within 30 min after finishing, have a snack that is 80% carbohydrate/20% protein (Endurox R4 is best).

- If you can soak your legs in cool water, during the first two hours after the race, do so.

- Walk for 20-30 minutes later in the day.

The next day

- Walk for 30-60 minutes, very easy. This can be done at one time, or in installments.

- Keep drinking about 4-6 oz an hour of water or sports drink like Accelerade.

- Wait at least a week before you either schedule your next race or vow to never run another one again.

Where to find out about races

Running stores

This resource is at the top of our list because you can usually get entry forms plus some editorial comment about the race. Explain to the store folks what you want to do in the race (competition for a certain time), etc. They will probably ask you for your projected finish time (or goal time). The more service-oriented store staff will look over the race choices to find a race that should have a good number of people to pull you along at that pace.

Friends who run

Call a friend who has run for several years. Tell him or her that you are looking for a race that is well organized, and accurately measured. Be sure to ask the friend for a contact number or website where you can find more information on the event, and possibly enter. As with running store folks, the editorial comments and evaluation of an event can steer you to a good experience.

Running clubs

If there is a running club or two in your area, get in touch. The officers or members can help you "match up" with an event for your time goal. Running clubs may be found by doing a web search: type "running clubs (your town)." The RRCA (Road Runner's Club of America) is a national organization of neighborhood clubs. From their website, search for a club in your area.

Newspaper listings

In many newspapers, there is a listing of community sports events, in the weekend section. This comes out on Friday or Saturday in most cities, usually in the lifestyle section. Some listings can be in the sports section under "running" or "road races." You can often find these listings on the website of the local newspaper.

Web searches

Just do a web search for "road races (your town)" or "5K (your town)." There are several event companies that serve as a registration center for many races: including www.signmeup.com & www.active.com From these sites you can sometimes find an event in your area, research it, and then sign up.

How to register

1. Online. More and more of the road running events are conducting registration online. This allows you to bypass the process of finding an entry form. This format makes it easier to enter before the deadline.

2. If mailing: Fill out an entry and send it in. You will need to fill out your name, address, T-shirt size, etc, and then sign the waiver form. Be sure to include a check for the entry fee.

3. Show up on race day. Because some races don't do race day registration, be sure that you can do this. There is usually a penalty for waiting until the last minute—but you can see what the weather is like before you make the trek to the race.

MENTAL

TOUGHNESS

Bottom line:
Motivational training can give you control over your attitude. This is what makes runners mentally tough.

Left brain vs right brain

The brain has two hemispheres that are separated and don't interconnect. The logical left brain does our business activities, trying to steer us into pleasure and away from discomfort. The creative and intuitive right side is an unlimited source of solutions to problems and connects us to hidden strengths.

As we accumulate stress, the left brain sends us a stream of messages telling us to "slow down," "stop and you'll feel better," "this isn't your day," and even philosophical messages like "why are you doing this." We are all capable of staying on track, and even pushing to a higher level of performance—even when the left brain is saying these things. So the first important step in taking command over motivation is to ignore the left brain unless there is a legitimate reason of health or safety (very rare), or, in fact, you are running a lot faster than you are ready to run. You can deal with the left brain, through a series of mental training drills.

Three strategies for staying mentally tough: Rehearsal, magic words, dirty tricks

These allow the right side of the brain to work on solutions to current problems. As the negative messages spew out of the left brain, the right brain doesn't argue. By preparing mentally for the challenges you expect, in three different ways, you will empower the right brain to deal with the problems and to develop mental toughness. Meanwhile the body gets the job done. But even more important, you will have three strategies for success.

I. Rehearsing success

Rehearsals develop patterns of thinking that get you in the groove for the behaviors you need to do. In a challenging situation, you don't want to have to think about the stress or the challenge but instead, take the right action, and move from one behavior to the next. The power of the rehearsal is that you have formatted your brain for a series of actions so that you don't have to think—and the sequence becomes almost automatic. By repeating the pattern, and adjusting, you'll revise it for real life, and can become the successful runner you want to be!

Drill # 1

Getting out the door after a hard day

By rehearsing yourself through a motivation problem, you can be more consistent and set the stage to improve. You must first have a goal that is do-able, and a rehearsal situation that is realistic. Let's learn by doing:

1. State your desired outcome: To be running from my house after a hard day.

2. Detail the challenge: Low blood sugar and fatigue, a stream of negative messages, need to get the evening meal ready to be cooked, overwhelming desire to feel relaxed.

3. Break up the challenge into a series of actions, which lead you through the mental barriers, no one of which is challenging to the left brain.

    • You're driving home at the end of the day, knowing that it is your workout day but you have no energy.

    • Your left brain says: "You're too tired" "take the day off" "You don't have the energy to run."

    • So you say to the left brain: "I'm not going to exercise. I'll put on some comfortable shoes and clothes, eat and drink, get food preparation going for dinner, and feel relaxed.

    • You're in your room, putting on comfortable clothes and shoes (they just happen to be used for running).

- You're drinking coffee (tea, diet cola, etc) and eating a good tasting energy snack, as you get the food prepared to go into the oven.

- Stepping outside, you check on the weather.

- You're walking to the edge of your block to see what the neighbors are doing.

- As you cross the street, you're on your way. The endorphins are kicking in, you feel good, you want to continue.

4. Rehearse the situation over and over, fine-tuning it so that it becomes integrated into the way you think and act—and reflects the specific situation that you will encounter in your race.

5. Finish by mentally enjoying the good feelings experienced with the desired outcome. You have felt the good attitude, the vitality, the glow from a good run-walk, and you are truly relaxed. So revisit these positive feelings at the end of each rehearsal.

Drill # 2

Getting out the door early in the morning

The second most common motivational problem that I'm asked about relates to the comfort of the bed, when you wake up and know that it is time to run.

State your desired outcome: To be walking and running away from the house early in the morning.

Detail the challenge: Desire to lie in bed, no desire to exert yourself so early. The stress of the alarm clock, and having to think about what to do next when the brain isn't working very fast.

Break up the challenge into a series of actions, which lead you through the mental barriers, no one of which is challenging to the left brain.

- The night before, you lay out your running clothes and shoes, near your coffee pot, so that you don't have to think.
- Set your alarm, and say to yourself over and over: "alarm off, feet on the floor, to the coffee pot" or…. "alarm, floor, coffee." As you repeat this, you visualize doing each action without thinking. By repeating it, you lull yourself to sleep. You have also been programming yourself for taking action the next morning.
- The alarm goes off. You shut it off, put feet on the floor, and you head to the coffee pot—all without thinking.
- You're putting on one piece of clothing at a time, sipping coffee, never thinking about exercise.

- With coffee cup in hand, you walk out the door to see what the weather is like.
- Sipping coffee, you walk to edge of your block or property to see what the neighbors are doing.
- Putting coffee down, you cross the street, and you have made the break!
- The endorphins are kicking in, you feel good, you want to continue.

Drill # 3

Pushing past the fatigue point where you tend to slow down

You're into a hard workout or race, and you are really tired. Your left brain is telling you that you can't reach your goal today, "just slow down a little, there are other days to work hard."

Evaluate whether there is a real medical reason why you can't run as projected. If there is a reason, back off and conserve—there will be another day.

Almost every time, however, the problem is more simple: you are not willing to push through the discomfort. The most effective way of getting tough mentally is to gradually push back your limits. Speed training programs can help you greatly. As you add to the number of repetitions, each week, you'll work on the mind as the body gets all systems working together to run faster.

Don't quit! Mental toughness can be as simple as not giving up. Just ignore the negative messages, and stay focused to the finish. If you've trained adequately, hang on and keep going.

In your speed workouts, practice the following drill. Fine-tune this so that when you run your goal race, you will have a strategy for staying mentally tough.

The scene:
You're getting very tired, you'd really like to call it quits, or at least slow down significantly.

Quick strategies:

Break up the remaining workout or race into segments that you know you can do:

- "1 more minute" Run for one minute, then reduce pace slightly for 10 seconds, then say "1 more minute" again, and again.
- "10 more steps" Run about 10 steps, take a couple of easy steps, then say "ten more steps."
- "One more step" Keep saying this over and over—you'll get there.

Take some shuffle breaks

- Reduce the tension on your leg muscles and feet by shuffling for a few strides every 1-2 minutes. By practicing "the shuffle", you'll find that you don't slow down much at all—while your muscles feel better.

Lap by lap, mile by mile

- In the workouts, start each lap saying to your self—"just one more" (even if you have 4 to go), or "I'll just run half a lap." You'll run the whole thing.

- In a track race, say "one more lap," or "one more half lap," or "just around the curve." In a road race, say "one more mile," "one more block," "just around the curve."

- When you are getting close to the end and really feel like you can't keep going, say to yourself "I am tough," or "I can endure," or "Yes I can."

II. Magic words

Even the most motivated person has sections during a tough workout or race when he or she wants to quit. By using a successful brainwashing technique, you can pull yourself through these negative thoughts, and feel like a champion at the end. On these days you have not only reached the finish line—you've overcome challenges to get there.

Think back to the problems that you face in your tough workouts or races. These are the ones that are most likely to challenge you again. As you go through a series of speed sessions and long runs, you will go through just about every problem you will face. Go back in your memory bank and pull out instances when you started to lose motivation due to these, but finished and overcame the challenge.

Relax.......Power.......Glide

In really tough runs, I have three challenges that occur over and over: 1) I become tense when I get really tired, worried that I will struggle badly at the end. 2) I feel the loss of the bounce and strength I had at the beginning, and worry that there will be no strength at the end. 3) My form starts to get ragged and I worry about further deterioration of muscles and tendons and more fatigue due to "wobbling".

Over the past three decades I have learned to counter these three problems with the magic words "Relax...Power....Glide". The visualization of each of these positives helps a little. The real magic comes from the association I have made with hundreds of successful experiences when I started to "lose it" in one of the three areas, but overcame the problems. Each time I "run through" one or more of the problems, I associate the experience with these magic words and add to the magic.

Now, when something starts to go wrong, I repeat the three words, over and over. Instead of increasing my anxiety, the repetition of the words calms me down. Even though I don't feel as strong at lap 5 as I did at lap one, I'm empowered just by knowing that I have a strategy and can draw upon my past experience. And when my legs lose the efficient path and bounce, I make adjustments and keep going.

When I say magic words that are associated with successful experience, there are two positive effects. The saying of the words floods the brain with positive memories. For a while, the negative messages of the left brain don't have a chance and I can get down the track for a lap or two (or the road for a mile or so). But the second effect may be more powerful. The words directly link you to the right brain, which works intuitively to make the same connections that allowed you solve the problems before.

To be successful on any day, you only need to finish the race. Most of the time, you can get through the "bad parts" by not giving up, and simply putting one foot in front of the other. If the body has done all of the training in this book, the weather is appropriate for your goal, and you are mentally prepared, you will push beyond the negative left brain messages during a series of workouts and earlier races. This develops the confidence to do this again, and again. Feel free to use my magic words, or develop your own. The more experiences you have associated with the words, the more magic they have.

III. Dirty tricks

The strategy of the rehearsal drill will get you focused and organized, while reducing the stress of the first few miles. Magic words will pull you along through most of the rest of the challenging sessions. But on the really rough days, it helps to have some tricks to play on the left side of the brain.

"Dirty Tricks" are quick fixes that distract the left brain for a while, allowing you to get down the road or the track for 300 yards or more. These imaginative and sometimes crazy images may not have any logic behind them. But when you counter a left brain message with a creative idea, you often confuse the left brain and stop the flow of negative messages.

The giant invisible rubber band

When I get tired on long or hard runs, I unpack this secret weapon, and throw it around someone ahead of me—or someone who had the audacity to pass me. For a while, the person doesn't realize that he or she has been "looped" and continues to push onward while I get the benefit of being pulled along. After a minute or two of mentally projecting myself into this image, I have to laugh for believing in such an absurd notion. But laughing activates the creative right side of the brain. This usually generates several more entertaining ideas, especially when you do this on a regular basis.

The right brain has millions of dirty tricks. Once you get it activated, you are likely to experience its solutions to problems you are currently having. It can entertain you as you get closer to your finish, step-by-step.

For many more dirty tricks and mental strategies, see *Galloway's Book On Running, 2nd Edition* and *Marathon— You Can Do It.*

CROSS TRAINING: GETTING BETTER AS YOU REST THE LEGS

The best item you can insert into a speed training program to reduce injury...is an extra rest day or two. The hard work of running involves lifting your body off the ground, and then absorbing the shock. If you are doing this every other day—even when doing speedwork—the limited damage can be repaired, and your fitness improved. Many runners—even in their 50s and 60s don't ever have injury layoffs when running every other day.

Once runners get into a speed program, and start to improve, some will try to sneak in an extra day or two on the days that should be "off." They often feel, mistakenly, that they can gain performance with an additional day; or that they are losing fitness when they take a day off. This perception does not match up with reality. Even with easy and short runs (on days that should be off) the legs cannot fully recover—especially from speed workouts. These short runs on rest days are the so-called "junk miles."

Cross training activities

The middle ground is to run one day, and cross-train the next. Cross training simply means "alternative exercise" to running. Your goal is to find exercises that give you a good feeling of exertion, but do not fatigue the workhorses of running: calf muscles, achilles tendon, feet.

The other exercises may not deliver the same good feelings—but they can come close. Many runners report that it may take a combination of 3 or 4 segments in a session to do this. But even if you don't feel exactly the same way, you'll receive the relaxation that comes from exercise, while you burn calories and fat.

When you are starting to do any exercise (or starting back, after a layoff):

1. Start with 5 easy minutes of exercise, rest for 20 or more minutes and do 5 more easy minutes.
2. Take a day of rest between this exercise (you can do a different exercise the next day).
3. Increase by 2-3 additional minutes each session until you get to the number of minutes that gives you the appropriate feeling of exertion.
4. Once you have reached two 15 minute sessions, you could shift to one 22-25 minute session and increase by 2-3 more minutes per session if you wish.
5. It's best to do no exercise the day before a long run, a very hard speed session, or a race.
6. To maintain your conditioning in each alternative exercise, do one session each week of 10 minutes or more once you reach that amount. If you have the time, you can cross-train (XT) on all of your days off from running—except listed in #5 above.
7. The maximum cross training is up to the individual. As long as you are feeling fine for the rest of the day and having no trouble with your runs the next day, the length of your cross training should not be a problem.

Water running can improve your running form

All of us have little flips and side motions of our legs that interfere with our running efficiency. During a water running workout, the resistance of the water forces your legs to find a more efficient path. In addition, several leg muscles are strengthened which can help to keep your legs on a smoother path when they get tired at the end of a long run.

Here's how!

You'll need a flotation belt for this exercise. The product "aqua jogger" is designed to float you off the bottom of the pool, and on most runners, tightens so that it is close to the body. There are many other ways to keep you floating, including water ski float belts and life jackets.

Get in the deep end of the pool and move your legs through a running motion. This means little or no knee lift, kicking out slightly in front of you, and bringing the leg behind, with the foot coming up behind you. As in running, your lower leg should be parallel with the horizontal during the back-kick.

If you are not feeling much exertion, you're probably lifting the knees too high and moving your legs through a small range of motion. To get the benefit, an extended running motion is needed.

It's important to do water running once a week to keep the adaptations that you have gained. If you miss a week, you should drop back a few minutes from your previous session. If you miss more than 3 weeks, start back at two 5-8 min sessions.

Fat burning and overall fitness exercises

Nordic track

This exercise machine simulates the motion used in cross country skiing. It is one of the better cross training modes for fat burning because it allows you to use a large number of muscle cells while raising body temperature. If you exercise at an easy pace, you can get into the fat burning zone (past 45 minutes) after a gradual build up to that amount. This exercise requires no pounding of the legs or feet and (unless you push it too hard or too long) allows you to run as usual the next day.

Rowing machine

There are a number of different types of rowing machines. Some work the legs a bit too hard for runners, but most allow you to use a wide variety of lower and upper body muscle groups. Like Nordic track, if you have the right machine for you, it's possible to continue to exercise for about as long as you wish, once you have gradually worked up to this. Most of the better machines are good fat-burners: they use a large number of muscle cells, raise temperature, and can be continued for more than three-quarters of an hour.

Cycling

Indoor cycling (on an exercise cycle) is a better fat burner exercise than outdoor cycling, because it raises your body temperature more—you don't get the cooling effect of the breeze that you generate on a bike. The muscles used in both indoor and outdoor cycling are mostly the quadraceps muscles—on the front of the thigh—reducing the total number of muscle cells compared with water running, nordic track, etc.

Don't forget walking!

Walking can be done all day long. I call walking a "stealth fat-burner" exercise because it is so easy to walk mile after mile—especially in small doses. But it is also an excellent cross training exercise—this includes walking on the treadmill. Caution: Don't walk with a long stride.

Cross training for the upper body

Weight training

While weight work is not a great fat-burning exercise, and does not directly benefit running, it can be done on non-running days, or on running days, after a run. There are a wide range of different ways to build strength. If interested, find a coach that can help you build strength in the muscle groups you wish to be strengthened. As mentioned previously in this book, weight training for the legs is not recommended.

Two postural strength exercises

The Crunch—lie on your back, on carpet or any padded surface. Lift your head and upper back slightly off the floor. Go through a narrow range of motion so that you feel your abdominal muscles contracting almost constantly. Start with a few seconds of these, and build up to 30-60 seconds, done 3-5 times a day (one or two days a week)

Arm running—while standing, with hand held weights (milk jugs, etc) move your arms through a wide range of motion you would use when running—maybe slightly more than usual. Keep the weights close to the body. Start with a few reps, and gradually build up to 3-5 sets of 10. Pick a weight that is challenging enough so that you feel exertion at the end of a set of 10. You don't want to have to struggle during the last few reps.

Note:
I do two exercises that have helped me maintain the strength of my postural muscles.

Swimming

While not a fat-burner, swimming strengthens the upper body, while improving cardiovascular fitness and endurance in those muscles. Swimming can be done on both running days and non-running days.

Push-ups and pull-ups

These can build great upper body strength as you innovate to work the upper body muscle groups you want to strengthen. If interested, see a strength expert for these variations.

Don't do these on non-running days!

The following exercises will tire the muscles used for running and keep them from recovering between run days. If you really like to do any of these exercises, you can do them after a run, on a short running day.

- Stair machines
- Stair aerobics
- Weight training for the leg muscles
- Power walking—especially on a hilly course
- Spinning classes (on a bicycle) in which you stand up on the pedals and push

Cross training can keep you fit, if you must stop running

I know of many runners who have had to take 2 weeks off from running or more, and have not lost noticeable fitness. How? They cross trained. As noted above, the most effective cross training mode is water running.

The key is to do an activity (like water running) that uses the same range of motion used in running. This keeps the neuromuscular system working to capacity.

To maintain conditioning, you must simulate the time and the effort level you would have spent when running. For example, if you were scheduled for a long run that would have taken you 60 minutes, get in the pool and run for 60 minutes. You can take segments of 30-40 seconds in which you reduce your effort (like a walk break), every few minutes, to keep the muscles resilient.

On a speed day, run water segments of about the same duration and intensity you would have run for those segments on the track. Whether going long or fast, try to get up to the same approximate respiration rate that you would have felt when running.

TOYS: HEART MONITORS AND GPS DEVICES

Heart monitors

Left brain runners who are motivated by technical items and data tracking, tell me that they are more motivated when using a heart monitor. Right brain runners who love the intuitive feel of running, find that the after-workout number crunching is often too intense, jolting them out of their transcendental state of running. But after talking with hundreds of both types of runners I realize that there are benefits—especially for runners who are doing speed training.

Once you determine your maximum heart rate, a good heart monitor can help you manage effort level. This will give you more control over the amount of effort you are spending in a workout, so that you can reduce overwork and recovery time. As they push into the exertion zone needed on a hard workout, left brain runners will gain a reasonably accurate reading on how much effort to spend or how much they need to back off to avoid a long recovery. Many "type A" runners have to be told to back off before they injure themselves. I've heard from countless numbers of these runners who feel that the monitors pay for themselves by telling them exactly how slow to run on easy days and how long to rest between speed repetitions during workouts. Right brain runners admit that they enjoy getting verification on the intuitive evaluation of effort levels. Bottom line is that monitors can tell you to go slow enough to recover, how long to rest during a speed session, and what your "red zone" is during a hard speed workout.

All devices have their "technical difficulties." Heart monitors can be influenced by local electronic transmissions, and mechanical issues. Cell phone towers and even garage doors can interfere with a monitor on occasion. This is usually a incidental issue. But if you have an abnormal reading either high or low, it may be a technical abnormality.

Be sure to read the instruction manual thoroughly—particularly about how to attach the device to your body for the most accurate reading. If not attached securely you will miss some beats. This means that you are actually working a lot harder than you think you are.

I suggest that you keep monitoring how you feel, at each 5% percentage increase toward max heart rate. Over time, you will get better at the intuitive feel, for example, of an 85% effort when you should be at 80%.

Get tested to determine max heart rate

If you are going to use a heart monitor, you should be tested to find your maximum heart rate. Some doctors (especially cardiologists) will do this. Other testing facilities include Human Performance Labs at Universities, and some health clubs and YMCAs. It is best to have someone supervising the test who is trained in cardiovascular issues. Sometimes the testing facility will misunderstand what you want. Be sure to say that you only need a "max heart rate test"—not a maximum oxygen uptake test. Once you have run for a couple of months with the monitor, you will have a clear idea what your max heart rate is from looking at your heart rate during a series of hard runs. Even on the hard speed workouts you can usually sense whether you could have worked yourself harder. But until you have more runs that push you to the limits, assume that your current top heart rate is within a beat or two of your current max that has been previously recorded.

Use the percentage of max heart rate as your standard

In general you don't want to get above 90% of max heart rate during workouts. At the end of a long training program, this may happen at the end of a speed workout or two—and only for a short period. But your goal is to keep the percentage between 70% and 80% during the first half of the speed workout or longer run, and minimize the upward drift at the end of the workout.

Computing max heart rate percentage

For example, if your max heart rate is 200

> 90% is 180
>
> 80% is 160
>
> 70% is 140
>
> 65% is 130

On easy days, stay below 65% of max heart rate

When in doubt, run slower. One of the major reasons for fatigue, aches and pains and burnout, is not running slowly enough on the recovery and fun days. Most commonly, the rate will increase at the end of a run. If this happens, slow down and take more walk breaks to keep it below 65%.

Between speed repetitions, let the pulse rate drop below 65% of max before doing another rep

To reduce the "lingering fatigue" that may continue for days after a hard workout, extend the rest interval walk until the heart rate goes down to this 65% level or lower. At the end of the workout, if the heart rate does not drop below this level for 5 minutes, you should do your warmdown and call it a day—*even if you have a few repetitions to go.*

Run smoother on speed repetitions so that your heart rate stays below 80% during speedwork

If you really work on running form improvements, you can minimize the heart rate increase by running more efficiently: keeping feet low to the ground, using a light touch, maintaining quick but efficient turnover of the feet. For more info on this, see the running form chapter in this book, or *Galloway's Book On Running, 2nd Edition*.

Morning pulse

If the chest strap doesn't interfere with your sleep, you can get a very accurate reading on your resting pulse in the morning. This will allow you to monitor over-training. Record the low figures each night. Once you establish a baseline, you should take an easy day when the rate rises 5%-9% above this. When it reaches 10% or above, you should take an extra day off. Even if the heart rate increase is due to an infection, you should not run unless cleared by your doctor.

Use the "two minute rule" for the pace of long runs—not heart rate

Even when running at 65% of max heart rate, many runners will be running a lot faster than they should at the beginning of long runs. Read the guidelines in this book for pacing the long runs, and don't be bashful about running slower.

But at the end of long runs, back off when heart rate exceeds 70% of max

There will be some upward drift of heart rate, due to fatigue at the end of long runs. Keep slowing down if this happens, so that you stay around 70% of max HR, or lower—even during the last few miles.

GPS and other distance-pace calculators

There are two types of devices for measuring distance, and both are usually very accurate: GPS and accelerometer technology. While some devices are more accurate than others, most will tell you, almost exactly how far you have run. This provides the best pacing feedback I know of—except for running on a track—so that you don't start your runs too fast, etc.

Using the more accurate products gives you freedom. You can do your long runs without having to measure the course, or being forced to run on a repeated, but measured, loop. Instead of going to a track to do speed sessions, you can very quickly measure your segments on roads, trails or residential streets with GPS devices. If your goal race is on the track, I recommend that at least half of your speed sessions be run on the track. This relates to the principle of training called "specificity."

The GPS devices track your movements by the use of navigational satellites. In general, the more satellites, the more accurate the measurement. There are "shadows" or areas of buildings, forest, or mountains in many areas where the signal cannot be acquired for (usually) short distances. You can see how accurate they are by running around a standard track. If you run in the middle of the first lane (not right next to the inside) you will be running about 0.25 mile.

The accelerometer products require a very easy calibration and have been shown to be very accurate. I've found it best on the calibration, to use a variety of paces and a walk break or two in order to simulate what you will be doing when you run.

Some devices require batteries, and others can be re-charged. It helps to go to a technical running store for advice on these products. The staff there can often give you some "gossip" on the various brands and devices from the feedback they receive about how they perform in real life.

"Forget about a personal record when it's over 60°F"

DEALING
WITH THE HEAT

If you slow down a little, on a warm day, you can finish strong, with a higher finish place. That seems obvious, but some runners "lose it" at the beginning of a hot race. The result is a much slower time—because of the inevitable slowdown at the end. For every second you run too fast during the first mile of a race on a hot day, you can usually expect to run 2-10 seconds slower at the end.

When you exercise strenuously in even moderate heat (above 60°F), you raise core body temperature. Most beginning runners will see the internal temperature rise above 55°F. This triggers a release of blood into the capilliaries of your skin to help cool you down.

This diversion, reduces the blood supply available to your exercising muscles, meaning that you will have less blood and less oxygen delivered to the power source that moves you forward—and less blood to move out the waste products from these work sites. As the waste builds up in the muscle, you will slow down.

So the bad news is that in warm weather you are going to feel worse and run slower. The worse news is that working too hard on a hot day could result in a very serious condition called heat disease. Make sure that you read the section on this health problem at the end of this chapter.

The good news is that you can adapt to these conditions to some extent, as you learn the best time of the day, clothing, and other tricks to keep you cool. But it is always better to back off or stop running at the first sign that you may be coming into this condition. The following are proven ways of avoiding heat adversity.

Running the long workouts during summer heat

1. Run before the sun gets above the horizon. Get up early during the warm months and you will avoid most of the dramatic stress from the sun. This is particularly a problem in humid areas. Early morning is usually the coolest time of the day, also. Without having to deal with the sun, most runners can gradually adapt to heat. At the very least, your runs will be more enjoyable than later in the day. Note: be sure to take care of safety issues.

2. If you must run when the sun is up, pick a shady course. Shade provides a significant relief in areas of low humidity, and some relief in humid environments.

3. In areas of low humidity, it's usually cool during the evening and night. In humid environments there may not be much relief. The coolest time of the day when it's humid, is just before dawn.

4. Have an indoor facility available. With treadmills, you can exercise in air conditioning. If a treadmill bores you, alternate segments of 5-10 minutes—one segment outdoor, and the next indoor.

5. Don't wear a hat! You lose most of your body heat through the top of your head. Covering the head will cause a quicker internal build-up of heat.

6. Wear light clothing, but not cotton. Many of the new, technical fibers (polypro, coolmax, drifit, etc) will move moisture away from your skin, producing a cooling effect. Cotton soaks up the sweat, making the garment heavier as it sticks to your skin. This means that you

won't receive as much of a cooling effect as that provided by the tech products.

7. Pour water over your head. Evaporation not only helps the cooling process—it makes you feel cooler. This offers a psychological boost which can be huge. If you can bring along ice water with you, you will feel a lot cooler as you squirt some regularly over the top of your head—using a pop top water bottle.

8. Do your short runs in installments. It is fine, on a hot day that is scheduled for an easy run, to put in your 30 minutes by doing 10 in the morning, 10 at noon and 10 at night. The long run, however, should be done at one time. Speed workouts should also be done all at once, but you may take more rest between speed reps, and you may break up the distance when it's hot (running twice as many 800s as one mile repeats).

9. Take a pool break, or a shower chill-down. During a run, it really helps to take a 2-4 minute dip in a pool or a shower. Some runners in hot areas run loops around their neighborhood and let the hose run over the head each lap. The pool is especially helpful in soaking out excess body temperature. I have run in 97 degree temperatures at our Florida running retreat, breaking up a 5 mile run into 3 x 1.7 mi. Between each, I take a 2-3 minute "soak break" and get back out there. It was only at the end of each segment that I got warm again.

10. Sun Screen—a mixed review. Some runners will need to protect themselves. Some products, however, produce a coating on the skin, slowing down the perspiration and producing an increase in body temperature build-up. If

you are only in the sun for 30-50 minutes at a time, you may not need to put on sunscreen for cancer protection. Consult with a dermatologist for your specific needs—or find a product that doesn't block the pores.

11. Drink 6-8 oz of a sports drink like Accelerade or water, at least every 2 hours, or when thirsty, throughout the day during hot weather.

12. Look at the clothing thermometer at the end of this section. Wear loose fitting garments, that have some texture in the fabric. Texture will limit or prevent the perspiration from causing a clinging and sticking to the skin.

13. When the temperature is above 90°F, you have my permission to re-arrange your running shoes— preferably in an air conditioned environment.

Hot weather slowdown for long runs

As the temperature rises above 55°F, your body starts to build up heat, but most runners aren't significantly slowed until 60°F. If you make the adjustments early, you won't have to suffer later and slow down a lot more at that time. The baseline for this table is 60°F or 14°C.

Between 60°F and 64°F —	slow down 30 seconds per mile slower than you would run at 60°F
Between 14°C and 16.5°C—	slow down 20 seconds per kilometer than you would run at 14°C
Between 65°F and 69°F —	slow down one minute per mile slower than you would run at 60°F
Between 17°C and 19.5°C—	slow down 40 seconds per kilometer slower than you would run at 14°C
Between 70°F and 74°F —	slow down 1:30/mile slower than you would run at 60°F
Between 20°C and 22°C —	slow down one minute/kilometer slower than you would run at 14°C
Between 75°F and 79°F —	slow down 2 min/mi slower than you would run at 60°F
Between 22.5°C and 25°C—	slow down 1:20/km slower than you would run at 14°C
Above 80°F and 25°C —	be careful, take extra precautions to avoid heat disease

Or....exercise indoors

Or....arrange your shoes next to the air conditioner

Heat disease alert!

While it is unlikely that you will push yourself into heat disease, the longer you are exercising in hot (and/or humid) conditions, the more you increase the likelihood of this dangerous medical situation. That's why I recommend breaking up your exercise into short segments when it's hot, if you must run outdoors. Be sensitive to your reactions to the heat, and those of the runners around you. When one of the symptoms is present, this is normally not a major problem unless there is significant distress. But when several are experienced, take action because heat disease can lead to death. It's always better to be conservative: stop the workout and cool off.

Symptoms:

- Intense heat build-up in the head
- General overheating of the body
- Significant headache
- Significant nausea
- General confusion and loss of concentration
- Loss of muscle control
- Excessive sweating and then cessation of sweating
- Clammy skin
- Excessively rapid breathing
- Muscle cramps
- Feeling faint
- Unusual heart beat or rhythm

Risk factors:

- Viral or bacterial infection
- Taking medication—especially cold medicines, diruretics, medicines for diarrhea, antihistamines,

atropine, scopolamine, tranquilizers, even cholesterol and blood pressure medications. Check with your doctor on medication issues—especially when running in hot weather.

- Dehydration (especially due to alcohol)
- Severe sunburn
- Overweight
- Lack of heat training
- Exercising more than one is used to
- Occurrence of heat disease in the past
- Two or more nights of extreme sleep deprivation
- Certain medical conditions including high cholesterol, high blood pressure, extreme stress, asthma, diabetes, epilepsy, cardiovascular disease, smoking, or a general lack of fitness
- Drug use, including alcohol, over-the-counter medications, prescription drugs, etc. (consult with your doctor about using drugs when you are exercising hard in hot weather)

Take action! Call 911

Use your best judgement, but in most cases anyone who exhibits two or more of the symptoms should get into a cool environment, and get medical attention immediately.

An extremely effective cool off method is to soak towels, sheets or clothing in cool or cold water, and wrap them around the individual. If ice is available, sprinkle some ice over the wet cloth.

Heat adaptation workout

If you regularly force yourself to deal with body heat build-up, your body will get better at running closer to your potential when hot. As with all training components, it is important to do this regularly. You should be sweating to some extent at the end of the workout, although the amount and the duration of perspiration is an individual issue. If the heat is particularly difficult, cut back the amount. Don't let yourself get into the beginning stages of heat disease. Get doctor's clearance before doing this.

Important note: Read the section on heat disease and stop this workout if you sense that you are even beginning to become nauseous, lose concentration or mental awareness of your condition, etc.

- Done on a short running day once a week.
- Do the run-walk ratio that you usually use, going at a very easy pace.
- Warm up with a 5 min walk and take a 5 min walk warmdown.
- Temperature should be between 75°F and 85°F (22-27°C) for best results.
- Stop at the first sign of nausea or significant heat stress, or other symptoms of heat disease.
- When less than 70°F (19°C), you can put on additional layers of clothing to simulate a higher temperature.
- First session, run-walk for only 3-4 minutes in the heat
- Each successive session, add 2-3 minutes.
- Build up to a maximum of 25 minutes—but don't push into heat disease.
- Regularity is important to maintain adaptations—once every week.
- If you miss a week or more, reduce the amount significantly and rebuild.

Tip: Maintaining heat tolerance during the winter

By putting on additional layers of clothing so that you sweat within 3-4 minutes of your run-walk, you can keep much of your summer heat conditioning—that took so much work to produce. Continue to run for a total of 12 minutes or more as you build according to the sidebar above.

TROUBLE-SHOOTING PERFORMANCE

Times are slowing down at end

- Your long runs aren't long enough
- You are running too fast at the beginning of the race
- You may benefit from walk breaks that are taken more frequently
- You may be overtrained—back off the speed sessions for a week or two
- In track workouts, run hardest at the end of the workout
- Temperature and/or humidity may be to blame—try slowing down at the beginning

Slowing down in the middle of the race

- You may be running too hard at the beginning—slow down by a few seconds each lap
- You may benefit from more frequent walk breaks
- In track workouts, work the hardest in the middle of the workout

Nauseous at the end

- You ran too fast at the beginning
- Temperature is above 65°F/17°C
- You ate too much (or drank too much) before the race or workout—even hours before
- You ate the wrong foods—most commonly, fat, fried foods, milk products, fibrous foods

Tired during workouts

- Low in B vitamins
- Low in iron—have a serum ferritin test
- Not eating enough protein

- Blood sugar is low before exercise
- Not eating within 30 min of the finish of a run
- Eating too much fat—especially before or right after a run
- Running too many days per week
- Running too hard on long runs
- Running too hard on all running days
- Not taking enough walk breaks from the beginning of your runs

PROBLEMS & SOLUTIONS

Side pain

This is very common, and usually has a simple fix. Normally it is nothing to worry about...it just hurts. This condition is due to 1) the lack of deep breathing, and 2) going a little too fast from the beginning of the run. You can correct #2 easily by walking more at the beginning, and/or slowing down your running pace during the first few minutes of running.

Tip:

Some runners have found that side pain goes away if they tightly grasp a rock in the hand that is on the side of the pain. Squeeze it for 15 seconds or so. Keep squeezing 3-5 times as you breathe deeply.

Deep breathing from the beginning of a run can prevent side pain. This way of inhaling air is performed by diverting the air you breathe into your lower lungs. Also called "belly breathing," this is how we breathe when asleep, and it provides maximum opportunity for oxygen absorption. If you don't deep breathe when you run, and you are not getting the oxygen you need, the side pain will tell you. By slowing down, walking, and breathing deeply for a while, the pain may go away. But sometimes it does not. Most runners just continue to run and walk with the side pain. In 50 years of running and helping others run, I've not seen any lasting negative effect from those who run with a side pain—it just hurts.

Note:

Never breathe in and out rapidly. This can lead to hyperventilation, dizziness, and fainting.

You don't have to take in a maximum breath to perform this technique. Simply breathe a normal breath but send it to the lower lungs. You know that you have done this if your stomach goes up and down as you inhale and exhale. If your chest goes up and down, you are breathing shallowly.

I feel great one day...and not the next

If you can solve this problem, you could become a very wealthy person. There are a few common reasons for this, but there will always be "those days" when the body doesn't seem to work right, or the gravity seems heavier than normal—and you cannot find a reason. You should keep looking for the causes of this, in your journal. If you feel this way several times a week, for two or more weeks in a row, you may need more rest in your program.

1. Just do it. In most cases, this is a one-day occurrence. Most runners just put more walking into the mix, slow down, and get through it. Before doing a speed workout, however, make sure that there's not a medical reason for the "bad" feeling. I've had some of my best workouts after feeling very bad during the first few miles—or the first few speed repetitions.

2. Heat and/or humidity will make you feel worse. You will often feel better when the temperature is below 60°F and miserable when 75°F or above—and/or the humidity is high.

3. Low blood sugar can make any run a bad run. You may feel good at the start and suddenly feel like you have no energy. Every step seems to take a major effort.

4. Low motivation. Use the rehearsal techniques in the "mental toughness" chapter to get you out the door on a bad day. These have helped numerous runners turn their minds around—even in the middle of a run.

5. Infection can leave you feeling lethargic, achy, and unable to run at the same pace that was easy a few days earlier. Check the normal signs (fever, chills, swollen lymph glands, higher morning pulse rate, etc.) and at least call your doctor if you suspect something.

6. Medication and alcohol, even when taken the day before, can leave a hangover that doesn't affect any area of your life except for your running. Your doctor or pharmacist should be able to tell you about the effect of medication on strenuous exercise.

7. A slower start can make the difference between a good day and a bad day. When your body is on the edge of fatigue or other stress, it only takes a few seconds too fast per mile, walking and/or running, to push into discomfort or worse. A quick adjustment to a slightly slower pace before you get too tired can turn this around.

8. Caffeine can help because it gets the central nervous system working to top capacity. I feel better and my legs work so much better when I have had a cup of coffee an hour before the start of a run. Of course, those who have any problems with caffeine should avoid it—or consult a doctor.

Cramps in the muscles

At some point, most people who run will experience an isolated cramp. These muscle contractions usually occur in the feet or the calf muscles and may come during a run or walk, or they may hit at random, afterward. Most commonly, they will occur at night, or when you are sitting around at your desk or watching TV in the afternoon or evening. When severe cramps occur during a run, you will have to stop or significantly slow down.

Cramps vary in severity. Most are mild but some can grab so hard that they shut down the muscles and hurt when they seize up. Massage, and a short and gentle movement of the muscle can help to bring most of the cramps around. Odds are that stretching will make the cramp worse, or tear the muscle fibers.

Most cramps are due to overuse—doing more than in the recent past, or continuing to put yourself at your limit, especially in warm weather. Look at the pace and distance of your runs and workouts in your training journal to see if you have been running too far, or too fast, or both.

- Continuous running increases cramping. Taking walk breaks more often can reduce or eliminate them. Several runners who used to cramp when they ran continuously, stopped cramping with a 10-30 second walk break each lap, or every 1-3 minutes during a long or fast run.
- During hot weather, a good electrolyte beverage (consumed during the day, throughout the day) can help to replace the salts that your body loses in sweating. A drink like Accelerade, for example, can help to top off these minerals when you drink about 6-8 oz every 1-2 hours, throughout the day.
- On very long hikes, walks or runs, however, the continuous sweating, especially when drinking a lot of fluid, can push your sodium levels too low and produce muscle cramping. If this happens regularly, a buffered salt tablet has helped greatly—a product like Succeed. If you have any blood pressure or other sodium issues, check with your doctor first.
- Many medications, especially those designed to lower cholesterol, have as one of their known side effects, muscle cramps. Runners who use medications and cramp should ask their doctor if there are alternatives.

Here are several ways of dealing with cramps:

1. Take a longer and more gentle warm-up
2. Shorten your run segment—or take walk breaks more often
3. Slow down your walk, and walk more
4. Shorten your distance on a hot/humid day
5. Break your run up into two segments (not on long runs or speed workouts)
6. Look at any other exercise that could be causing the cramps
7. Take a buffered salt tablet at the beginning of your exercise
8. Don't push off as hard, or bounce as high off the ground
9. During speed workouts on hot days, walk more during the rest interval

Note:

If you have high blood pressure or similar problem, ask your doctor before taking any salt product.

Upset stomach or diarrhea

Sooner or later, virtually every runner has at least one episode with nausea or diarrhea. It comes from the build-up of total stress that you accumulate in your life—and specifically the stress of the workout. But stress is the result of many unique conditions within the individual. Your body produces the nausea/diarrhea to get you to reduce the exercise, which will reduce the stress. Here are the common causes.

1. **Running too fast or too far** is the most common cause. Runners are confused about this, because the pace doesn't feel too fast in the beginning. Each person has a level of fatigue that triggers these conditions. Slowing down and taking more walk breaks will help you manage the problem. Speed training and racing will increase stress very quickly.

2. **Eating too much or too soon before the run.** Your system has to work hard when running, and it is also hard work to digest food. Doing both at the same time raises stress and results in nausea, etc. Having food in your stomach, in the process of being digested is an extra stress and a likely target for elimination.

3. **Eating a high fat or high protein diet.** Even one meal that has over 50% of the calories in fat or protein can lead to N/D hours later.

4. **Eating too much the afternoon or evening, the day before** A big evening meal will still be in the gut the next morning, being digested. When you bounce up and down on a run, which you will, you add stress to the system, sometimes resulting in nausea/diarrhea (N/D).

5. **Heat and Humidity** are a major cause of these problems. Some people don't adapt well to even modest heat increases and experience N/D when racing (or doing speed sessions) at the same pace that did not produce the problem in cool weather. In hot conditions, everyone has a core body temperature increase that will result in significant stress to the system—often causing nausea, and sometimes diarrhea. By slowing down, taking more walk breaks, and pouring water over your head, you can manage this better.

6. **Drinking too much water** *before* **a run.** If you have too much water in your stomach, and you are bouncing around, you put stress on the digestive system. Reduce your intake to the bare minimum. Most runners don't need to drink any fluid before a run that is 60 minutes or less.

7. **Drinking too much of a sugar/electrolyte drink.** Water is the easiest substance for the body to process. The addition of sugar and/or electrolyte minerals, as in a sports drink, makes the substance harder to digest. During a run (especially on a hot day) it is best to drink only water if you have had N/D or other problems. Cold water is best.

8. **Drinking too much fluid (especially a sugar drink) too soon** *after* **a run.** Even if you are very thirsty, don't gulp down large quantities of any fluid during a short period of time. Try to drink no more than 6-8 oz, every 20 minutes or so. If you are particularly prone to N/D, just take 2-4 sips, every 5 minutes or so. When the body is very stressed and tired, it's not a good idea to consume a sugar drink (sports drink, etc). The extra stress of digesting the sugar can lead to problems.

9. **Don't let running be stressful to you.** Some runners get too obsessed about getting their run in or running at a specific pace. This adds stress to your life. Relax and let your run diffuse some of the other tensions in your life. When you are under a lot of "life stress" it's OK to delay a speed workout when the thought of fast running seems to increase your stress level. Take an easy jog!

Headache

There are several reasons why runners get headaches on runs. While uncommon, they happen to the average runner about 1-5 times a year. The extra stress that running puts on the body can trigger a headache on a tough day—even considering the relaxation that comes from the run. Many runners find that a dose of an over-the-counter headache medication takes care of the problem. As always, consult with your doctor about use of medication. Here are the causes/solutions.

Dehydration—if you run in the morning, make sure that you hydrate well the day before. Avoid alcohol if you run in the mornings and have headaches. Also watch the salt in your dinner meal the night before. A good sports drink like accelerade, taken throughout the day the day before, will help to keep your fluid levels and your electrolytes "topped off". If you run in the afternoon, follow the same advice leading up to your run, on the day of the run. If you are dehydrated an hour before a run, it doesn't help to drink a huge amount of water at that time—6-8 oz is fine.

Medications can often produce dehydration—There are some medications that make runners more prone to headaches. Check with your doctor.

Too hot for you—run at a cooler time of the day (usually in the morning before the sun gets above the horizon). When on a hot run, pour water over your head.

Being in the sun. Try to stay in the shade as much as possible. Wear a visor not a hat, making sure the band is not too tight.

Running a little too fast—start all runs more slowly, walk more during the first half of the run

Running further than you have run in the recent past—monitor your mileage and don't increase more than about 15% further than you have run on any single run in the recent past.

Low blood sugar level—be sure that you boost your BLS with a snack, about 30-60 min before you run. If you are used to having it, caffeine in a beverage can sometimes help this situation also—but caffeine causes headaches for a small percentage of runners.

If prone to migranes—generally avoid caffeine, and try your best to avoid dehydration. Talk to your doctor about other possibilities.

Watch your neck and lower back—If you have a slight forward lean as you run, you can put pressure on the spine—particularly in the neck and lower back. Read the form chapter in this book and run upright.

INJURY TROUBLE-SHOOTING

Quick treatment tips

For all injuries:

1. Take 3 days off from running or any activity that could aggravate the area
2. Avoid any activity that could aggravate the injury
3. As you return to running, stay below the threshold of further irritation with much more liberal walking
4. Don't stretch unless you have ilio-tibial band injury. Stretching keeps most injuries from healing.

Muscle injuries:

1. Call your doctor's office and see if you can take prescription strength anti inflammatory medication.
2. See a sports massage therapist who has worked successfully on many runners.

Tendon and foot injuries

1. Rub a chunk of ice directly on the area for 15 minutes every night (keep rubbing until the area gets numb— about 15 minutes).

Note:
Ice bags, or gel ice don't seem to do any good at all

2. Foot injuries sometimes are helped by an air cast at first to let the problem start healing.

Knee injuries

1. Call your doctor's office to see if you can take prescription strength anti-inflammatory medication.
2. See if you can do a little gentle walking, sometimes this helps.

3. Sometimes the knee straps can relieve pain, ask your doctor.
4. Get a shoe check to see if you are in the right shoe (if you over-pronate, a motion control shoe may help).
5. If you over pronate, an orthotic may help.
6. If you have internal knee pain, glucosamine supplement, may help.

Shin injuries

1. Rule out a stress fracture. In this case, the pain usually gets worse as you run—but check with your doctor.
2. If the pain gradually goes away as you run on it, there is less worry of a stress fracture. This is probably a shin splint. If you stay below the threshold of irritating the shin muscle, you can run with shin splints as they gradually go away (check with doctor to be sure).
3. Take more walk breaks, run more slowly, etc.

Starting running before the injury has healed

With most running injuries, you can continue to run even while the injury is healing. But first, you must have some time off to get the healing started. If you do this at the beginning of an injury you will usually only need 2-5 days off. The longer you try to push through the problem, the more damage you produce and the longer it will take to heal. Stay in touch with the doc at any stage of this healing/running process, follow his/her advice, and use your best judgement.

To allow for healing, once you have returned to running, stay below the threshold of further irritation. In other words, if the injury feels a little irritated when running at

2.5 miles, and starts hurting a little at 3 miles, you should run no more than 2 miles. And if your run-walk ratio is 3 min run/1 min walk, you should drop back to 1-1 or 30 seconds/30 seconds.

Always allow a day of rest between running days. With most injuries you can cross train to maintain conditioning, but make sure that your injury will allow this. Again, your doctor can advise.

Best cross training modes to maintain your running conditioning

Before doing any of these ask your doctor. Most are fine for most injuries. But some run a risk of irritating the injured area and delaying the healing process. For more information on this, see the chapter on cross training, in my *Galloway's Book On Running, 2nd Edition*. Gradually build up the cross training, because you have to condition those muscles gradually also. Even walking is a great way to maintain conditioning if the injury and the doctor will allow it.

1. Running in the water—can improve your running form
2. Nordic Track machines
3. Walking
4. Rowing machines
5. Eliptical machines

There is much more information on specific injuries in my *Galloway's Book On Running, 2nd Edition*. But here are some helpful items that I want to pass on as one runner to another.

Treatment suggestions— from one runner to another

Knee pain

Most knee problems will go away if you take 5 days off. Ask your doctor if you can use anti-inflammatory medication. Try to figure out what caused the knee problem. Make sure that your running courses don't have a slant or canter. Look at the most worn pair of shoes you have, even walking shoes. If there is wear on the inside of the forefoot, you probably overpronate. If you have repeat issues with knee pain, you may need a foot support or orthotic. If there is pain under the kneecap, or arthritis, the glucosamine/chondroitin products have helped. The best I've found in this category is Joint Maintenance Product by Cooper Complete.

Outside of the pain—

Iliotibial Band Syndrome

This band of fascia acts as a tendon, going down the outside of the leg from the hip to just below the knee. The pain is most commonly felt on the outside of the knee, but can be felt anywhere along the I-T band. I believe this to be a "wobble injury." When the running muscles get tired, they don't keep you on a straight running track. The I-T band tries to restrain the wobbling motion, but it cannot and gets overused. Most of the feedback I receive from runners and doctors is that once the healing has started (usually a few days off from running), most runners will heal as fast when you run on it as from a complete layoff. It is crucial to stay below the threshold of further irritation.

Treatment for Ilio-tibial band:

1. Stretching: Stretch before, after, and even during a run. Here are several stretches that have worked for this injury.

2. Self-massage using a foam roller. This device has helped thousands of runners get over I-T band. On my website *www.RunInjuryFree.com* is a picture of someone using a foam roller. Put the roller on the floor, lie on it using body weight to press and roll the area that is sore. It helps to warm up the area before a run, and to roll it out afterward.

3. Massage Therapy: a good massage therapist can tell whether massage will help and where to massage. The two areas for possible attention are the connecting points of the connective tissue that is tight, and the fascia band itself, in several places. "The stick" is a self massage roller device that has also helped many runners recover from I-T band as they run. As with the foam roller, it helps to warm up the area before a run, and to roll it out afterward.

4. Walking is usually fine—and usually you can find a run-walk ratio that works.

5. Direct ice massage on the area of pain: 15 minutes of continuous rubbing every night.

Shin pain—"Shin Splints" or Stress Fracture

Almost always, pain in this area indicates a minor irritation called "shin splints" that allows running and walking as you heal. The greatest pain or irritation during injury is during the start of a run or walk, which gradually lessens or goes away as you run and walk. It takes a while to fully heal, so you must have patience.

Inside pain—posterior shin splints. Irritation of the inside of the leg, coming up from the ankle is called "posterior tibial shin splints" and is often due to over pronation of the foot (foot rolls in at pushoff).

Front of shin—anterior shin splints. When the pain is in the muscle on the front of the lower leg it is "anterior tibial shin splints". This is very often due to having too long a stride when running and especially when walking. Downhill terrain should be avoided as much as possible during the healing.

Stress fracture. If the pain is in a very specific place, and increases as you run, it could be a more serious problem: a stress fracture. This is unusual for beginning runners, but characteristic of those who do too much, too soon. It can also indicate low bone density. If you even suspect a stress fracture, do not run or do anything stressful on the leg and see a doctor. Stress fractures take weeks of no running and walking, usually wearing a cast. They may also indicate a calcium deficiency.

Heel pain—Plantar Fascia

"The most effective treatment is putting your foot in a supportive shoe before your 1st step in the morning"

This very common injury (pain on the inside or center of the heel) is felt when you first walk on the foot in the morning. As you get warmed up, it gradually goes away, only to return the next morning. The most important treatment is to put your foot in a supportive shoe, before you step out of bed. Be sure to get a "shoe check" at a technical running store to make sure that you have the right shoe for your foot. If the pain is felt during the day, and is painful, you should consult with a podiatrist. Usually the doctor will construct a foot support that will surround your arch and heel. This does not always need to be a hard orthotic and is usually a softer one designed for your foot with build-ups in the right places.

The "toe squincher" exercise noted in this book, can help develop foot strength that will also support the foot. It takes several weeks for this to take effect. This is another injury that allows for running as you heal, but stay in touch with your doctor.

Back of the foot—Achilles Tendon

The achilles tendon is the narrow band of tendon rising up from the heel and connecting to the calf muscle. It is part of a very efficient mechanical system, acting like a strong rubber band to leverage a lot of work out of the foot, with a little effort from the calf muscle. It is usually injured due to excessive stretching, either through running or through stretching exercises. First, avoid any activity that stretches the tendon in any way.

It helps to add a small heel lift to all shoes, which reduces the range of motion. Every night, rub a chunk of ice directly on the tendon. Keep rubbing for about 15 minutes, until the tendon gets numb. Bags of ice or frozen gels don't do any good at all in my opinion. Usually after 3-5 days off from running, the icing takes hold and gets the injury in a healing mode. My doctor friends tell me that achilles tendon injuries are rarely helped by anti-inflammatory medication.

Hip and groin pain

There are a variety of elements that could be aggravated in the hip area. Since the hips are not prime movers in running, they are usually abused when you continue to push on, after getting very tired. The hips try to do the work of the leg muscles and are not designed for this. Ask your doctor about prescription strength anti inflammatory medication, as this can often speed up recovery. Avoid stretching and any activity that aggravates the area.

Calf muscle

The calf is the most important muscle for running. It is often irritated by speedwork, and can be pushed into injury by stretching, running too fast when tired, by too many speed sessions without adequate rest between, and sprinting at the end of races or workouts.

Deep tissue massage has been the best treatment for most calf muscle problems. Try to find a very experienced massage therapist who has helped lots of runners with calf problems. This can be painful but is about the only way to remove some bio-damage in the muscle. The "stick" can be very beneficial for working damage out of the calf muscle— on a daily basis (see our website for more information on this product).

Don't stretch! Stretching will tear the muscle fibers that are trying to heal. Avoid running hills, and take very frequent walk breaks as you return to running.

THE CLOTHING THERMOMETER

After years of working with people in various climates, here are my recommendations for the appropriate clothing based upon the temperature. First, choose garments that will be comfortable—especially next to your skin, and especially at the end of a run. You may have to resist the temptation to buy a fashion color, but function is most important. Watch for seams and bunching up in areas where you will have body parts rubbing together, thousands of times during a run.

Cotton is usually not a good fabric for those who perspire a great deal. The cotton will absorb the sweat, hold it next to your skin, and increase the weight you must carry during the run. Garments made out of fabric labeled Polypro, Coolmax, Drifit, etc., hold enough body heat close to you in winter, while releasing extra heat. In summer and winter, they move moisture away from the skin—cooling you in hot weather, and avoiding a chill in the winter—and limiting the weight increase from perspiration.

Temperature	What to wear
14°C or 60°F and above	Tank top or singlet, and shorts
9 to13°C or 50 to 59°F	T-shirt and shorts
5 to 8°C or 40 to 49°F	Long sleeve light weight shirt, shorts or tights (or nylon long pants) Mittens and gloves
0 to 4°C or 30 to 39°F	Long sleeve medium weight shirt, and another T-shirt, tights and shorts, Socks or mittens or gloves and a hat over the ears

-4 to –1°C or 20-29°F	Medium weight long sleeve shirt, another T-shirt, tights and shorts, sox, mittens or gloves, and a hat over the ears
-8 to –3°C or 10-19°F	Medium weight long sleeve shirt, and medium/heavy weight shirt, Tights and shorts, nylon wind suit, top and pants, socks, thick mittens. And a hat over the ears
-12 to –7°C or 0-9°F	Two medium or heavyweight long sleeve tops, thick tights. Thick underwear (especially for men), Medium to heavy warm up, Gloves and thick mittens, ski mask, a hat over the ears, and Vaseline covering any exposed skin.
-18 to –11°C or –15°F	Two heavyweight long sleeve tops, tights and thick tights, thick underwear (and supporter for men), thick warm up (top and pants) mittens over gloves, thick ski mask and a hat over ears, vasoline covering any exposed skin, thicker socks on your feet and other foot protection, as needed.
Minus 20° both C & F	Add layers as needed

What not to wear

1. *A heavy coat in winter.* If the layer is too thick, you'll heat up, sweat excessively, and cool too much when you take it off.
2. *No shirt for men in summer.* Fabric that holds some of the moisture will give you more of a cooling effect as you run and walk.
3. *Too much sun screen*—it can interfere with sweating
4. *Sox that are too thick in summer.* Your feet swell and the pressure from the sox can increase the chance of a black toenail and blisters.
5. *Lime green shirt with bright pink polka dots* (unless you have a lot of confidence and/or can run fast).

Special cases:

Chaffing can be reduced by lycra and other fabric. Many runners have eliminated chaffing between the legs by using a lycra "bike tight" as an undergarment. These are also called "lycra shorts." There are several skin lubricants on the market, including Glide.

Some men suffer from irritation of their nipples. Having a slick and smooth fabric across the chest will reduce this. There is now a product called Nip-Guard that has allowed many men to completely avoid the problem.

PRODUCTS THAT ENHANCE RUNNING

The stick

This massage tool can help the muscles recover quicker. It will often speed up the recovery of muscle injuries or Iliotibial Band injuries (on the outside of the upper leg, between knee and hip). This type of device can help warm up the legs muscles and sore tendons (etc.) before running, and move some of the waste out afterward.

In working on the calf muscle (most important in running) start each stroke at the achilles tendon and roll up the leg toward the knee. Gently roll back to the origin and continue, repeatedly. For the first 5 minutes your gentle rolling will bring additional blood flow to the area. As you gradually increase the pressure on the calf you will usually find some "knots" or sore places in the muscles. Concentrate on these as you roll over them again and again, breaking up the tightness. See *www.RunInjuryFree.com* for more info on this.

Foam roller—self massage for I-T band, hip, etc.

The most popular size of this cylinder is about 6" in diameter and one foot long. This has been the most successful treatment device for Ilio-tibial band injury. In treating this injury, put the roller on the floor, and lie on your side so that the irritated I-T band area is on top of the roller. As your body weight presses down on the roller, roll up and down on the area of the leg you want to treat. Roll gently for 2-3 minutes and then let the body weight press down more.

This is a very effective pre-warm-up exercise for any area that needs more blood flow as you start. It is also very beneficial to use the roller after a run on the same areas. See *www.RunInjuryFree.com* for more info on this product.

Cryo-cup—best tool for ice massage

Rubbing with a chunk of ice on a sore area (when near the skin) Is very powerful therapy. I know of hundreds of cases of achilles tendon problems that have been healed by this method. The Cryo-Cup is a very convenient device for ice massage. The plastic cup has a plastic ring that sits on top of it. Fill it up with water, then freeze.

When you have an ache or pain, pour warm water over the cup to release it giving you an ice "popcicle". Rub for about 15 minutes, constantly moving it on the area, until the tendon (etc) is numb. When finished, fill up the cup again for use next time. It may surprise you, but rubbing with a plastic bag of ice—or a frozen gel product—does no good at all in most cases.

Endurox excel

An hour before a long or hard workout, I take two of these Excel pills. Among the anti-oxidants is the active ingredient from gensing: ciwujia. Research has shown that recovery speeds up when this product is taken. I also use it when my legs have been more tired than usual for 2-3 days in a row.

Accelerade

This sports drink has a patented formula shown to improve recovery. It also helps to improve hydration. I recommend having some in the refrigerator as your fluid intake product taken throughout the day. Prime time to drink this regularly is the day before and after a long or strenuous workout day. During a prolonged speed training session, have a thermos nearby, for sipping on walk breaks.

Research has also shown that drinking Accelerade about 30 min before running can get the body's startup fuel (glycogen) activated more effectively, and may conserve the limited supply of this crucial fuel.

Endurox R4

This product has what I see as a "cult following" among runners. In fact, the research shows that the 4-1 ratio of carbohydrate to protein helps to reload the muscle glycogen more quickly. This means that the muscles feel bouncy and ready to do what you can do, sooner. There are other anti-oxidants that speed recovery. Prime time for this re-loading process is within 30 minutes of the finish of a run.

Jeff Galloway's training journal

Some type of journal is needed to organize, and track, your year-round plan. My own product can be ordered from www.JeffGalloway.com, autographed. It simplifies the process, with places to fill in information for each day. Your journal allows you to organize your training in advance, which you can use as a daily workout guide. As you plan ahead and enter your data, you gain control over your training.

Other Galloway books

(for more information on these, see book section at *www.JeffGalloway.com*)

Getting Started: This book is targeted at beginners, so the training programs are more gentle than those in other books. It gently takes walkers into running, with the nutrition, motivation, and body management tips needed.

Testing Yourself: Training programs for 1 mile, 2 mile, 5K, and 1.5 mile are detailed, along with information on racing specific information in nutrition, mental toughness, running form. There are also some very accurate prediction tests that allow you to tell what is a realistic goal.

Galloway's Book On Running 2nd Edition: This is the best-seller among running books since 1984. Thoroughly revised and expanded in 2001, you'll find training programs for 5K, 10K, Half Marathon, with nutrition, fat-burning, walk breaks, motivation, injuries, shoes, age and maturity issues, and much more.

Marathon This has the latest information on training for the classic event. There are training programs, with details on walk breaks, long run and marathon nutrition, mental marathon toughness.

Vitamins

I now believe that most runners need a good vitamin to help the immune system and resist infection. There is some evidence that getting the proper vitamin mix can speed recovery. The vitamin line I use is called Cooper Complete. Dr. Kenneth Cooper, is behind this product. In the process of producing the best body of research on exercise and long-term health I've seen anywhere, he found that certain vitamins help in many ways.

Buffered salt tablets—to reduce cramping

If your muscles cramp on long or hard runs, this type of product may help greatly. The buffered sodium and potassium tablets get into the system more quickly. Be sure to ask your doctor if this product is OK for you (those with high blood pressure, especially). If you are taking a statin drug for cholesterol, and are cramping, it is doubtful that this will help. Ask your doctor about adjusting the medication before long runs.

Photo Credits

Cover Photo: Polar Electro

Cover Design: Jens Vogelsang

Inside Photos: Polar Electro
Andy Sharp